Judith

MAZILLI'S SHOES

*For the love
of fairness + justice .*

*[signature]
Jan /2014*

DRAMA SERIES 17

Guernica Editions Inc. acknowledges the support of
the Canada Council for the Arts.

Canadä

Guernica Editions Inc. acknowledges the financial support of
the Government of Canada through the Book Publishing Industry
Development Program (BPIDP).

DARLENE MADOTT

MAZILLI'S SHOES

A SCREENPLAY

GUERNICA
TORONTO·BUFFALO·LANCASTER (U.K.)
1999

Antonio D'Alfonso, editor
Guernica Editions Inc.
P.O. Box 117, Station P, Toronto (ON), Canada M5S 2S6
2250 Military Road, Tonawanda, N.Y. 14150-6000 U.S.A.
Gazelle, Falcon House, Queen Square, Lancaster LA1 1RN U.K.
Printed in Canada.

Legal Deposit — Fourth Quarter
National Library of Canada
Library of Congress Catalog Card Number: 99-64601
Canadian Cataloguing in Publication Data
Madott, Darlene
Mazilli's shoes
(Drama series ; 17)
Includes some text in Italian.
ISBN 1-55071-097-4
I. Title. II. Series.
PS8576.A335M39 1999 C812'.54 C99-900888-9
PR9199.3.M3424M39 1999

FOREWORD

During the research for *Mazilli's Shoes,* I told a man shooting pool in one of the cafés off Toronto's St. Clair Avenue that I was writing the story of a man who comes to Canada from Italy with the dream of making it rich here, so that he can go home again. The man shrugged his shoulders, as if to say, so what? What could possibly be different about this story he hadn't heard so many times before?

Yes, but while most immigrants lose sight of their dream, or realize en route its futility, Mazilli never lets go. Mazilli is a man who will not compromise or dilute the ultimate goal with the odd trip home to Italy.

Just as *The Odyssey* is about "the man of twists and turns/driven time and again off course/once he had plundered the hallowe'd heights of Troy," all journeys are not about the destination, but about the twists and turns that drive you continuously off course. If anything makes Mazilli's story a little different, it is this: Of the two worst things in life (never getting what you want; getting what you want) Mazilli discovers the latter.

At the comic centre of *Mazilli's Shoes* is the tragedy of a man who gets what he wants.

MAZILLI'S SHOES

Titles up and over the following: Toronto, off Caledonia, near Little Italy.

EXTERIOR (EXT.) SHOE FACTORY. WINTER MORNING.
The factory is an old, one-storey affair, with an unassuming entrance. Its weathered sign announces: Francine Footwear Limited. Its parking lot is runny with desultory March slush and banked with old snow.

INTERIOR (INT.) SHOE FACTORY.
Series of shots to create shoe-making process: workers cut, fit, last and package. Giovanni Mazilli, a strong-looking man in his late forties, strides down an assembly line; he pauses to point out something about a shoe in a worker's hands. His demeanour is authoritative, but an affectionate pat to the worker's shoulder and smiling acknowledgement from the worker indicate Giovanni is respected and well-liked. Whistle blows. The worker's steam press decompresses. Silence, as power in the factory is cut to the machines, replaced by rising buzz of voices. Giovanni and worker look up in surprise, as voice begins calling out names.

RECEIVER
Tony Falcone.
Another angle: the receiver in a business suit, flanked by two security guards, calls out names in a perfunctory voice. He is circled by workers, some reading the contents of their envelopes, others just opening them. Dismay and lack of comprehension all around.

Frank Lomangino.

> *As each name is called, a person steps forward to receive an envelope.*

Maria Minardo.

> *Giovanni appears in the circle. Some of the workers hold out their envelopes to him, as if for explanation. Giovanni moves through the circle of workers and confronts the suited man directly.*

GIOVANNI
With authority.
What is going on here?

RECEIVER
The plant is closed. You're getting your cheques for the last pay period, with severance.

GIOVANNI
What are you talking about? Where's Mr. Goldberg? Who are you?

RECEIVER
Who are you?

GIOVANNI
Giovanni Mazilli. Plant Manager. What's your name? You have a name?

SECURITY GUARD
Keep it down. There's no need to make trouble here.

GIOVANNI
Giovanni Mazilli doesn't make trouble. He asks questions. I asked you a question, Mr. No Name. I want an explanation.

> *Opening his arms to include his workers.*

We demand an explanation.

> *Workers voices rise in protest. The receiver cooly sorts through his envelopes until he finds the one he's looking for.*

RECEIVER

Giovanni Mazilli. Your explanation.

Close on Giovanni as, stunned, he receives his own envelope. Without reading it, holding the envelope like a baton in his fist, he takes off running. Security guard tries to grab his sleeve, as he passes.

SECURITY GUARD

Hey, you.

INT. CORRIDOR OF FACTORY. DAY.

Following on Giovanni, running down corridor, closely followed by security guard. Giovanni reaches a glassed-in office, its frosted door painted with the words Mr. Goldberg, President. Clutching the door handle, he tears it open.

INT. OFFICE. DAY.

The office has been emptied out, its 1950s yellow-oak desk top cleared; no coat on the rack; stained squares on the walls where pictures have been removed. Giovanni sees everything at a glance.
Close: Giovanni's face. He looks as if he has been slapped.

ESTABLISHING (EST.) LITTLE ITALY. EARLY AFTERNOON.

It's a slushy March day. Giovanni's station wagon travels along St. Clair in heavy traffic on a busy Friday afternoon. He is lost in thought — so lost that he stays parked when the light changes. The car behind him honks and passes him on the inside lane; its driver gives Mazilli the finger as he passes.

DRIVER

Where's your head?
[A che pensavi?]

EXT. BLUE BIRD CAFE, ST. CLAIR AVE. AFTERNOON.
*All the metered parking spaces are available in front of
the Blue Bird café. Giovanni makes a U-turn across St.
Clair Avenue, and parks immediately in front of the
Blue Bird window. He gets out and puts change into
the parking metre.*

INT. THE BLUE BIRD CAFÉ. DAY.
*The Blue Bird is a traditional Little-Italy bar, with
tables for cappuccino and cards in the front room and
a back room for billiards and video games. Scene opens
with the lupo (wolf) playing boccetta with his opponent while men watch and heckle from chairs ringing
the table. The wolf takes his shot and gives the wolf
howl that is his leitmotif. As his opponent prepares to
shoot, the Lupo clucks at him, as if to signify he's a
chicken the wolf is about to devour. Enter Giovanni
Mazilli.*

LUCIANO
Stops chalking his cue to check his watch.
Hey, Mr. Plant Manager, you on holiday today, or what?

GIOVANNI
Ignoring him.
Cuncetta, *una birra.*
*Cuncetta, the bar owner's wife, brings a beer to the
table where Giovanni paces restlessly, beside his cro-
nies, his back to the window that looks out upon St.
Clair Avenue and the station wagon. They are playing
scopa. Sonny throws out a card.*

SONNY
To no one in particular.
So what you think, Italy will clean up Tangentopoli?

PAPA
Italy without the Mafiosi is like Venice without the smell.

Papa raps his fingers on the table, impatient for Sonny to play his next card.

Luciano, enough with the cue.

Looking distractedly at Giovanni's pacing.

Everybody's nervous today. What's the matter, bad day at work?

GIOVANNI

Work? Not even the work was our own.

PAPA

What you talk about?

GIOVANNI

Twenty-three years, I'm talking about. The shoe factory. It closed today. *Finito.* Just like that.

LUCIANO
Stops chalking.

No shit.

The cronies stop their card game, all attention.

GIOVANNI

Mr. Goldberg isn't even there. Just Mr. Receiver, with his envelopes. An envelope for each of my workers. They look to me, but I have no explanation — just my own envelope.

SONNY

So how do you feel?

PAPA

Ciuccio, how do you think he feels?

LUCIANO

You'll get used to it. You're Italian, Italians can adopt to anything.

GIOVANNI

I trusted the man. His kid's first pair of shoes, I made! He can't tell me to my face?

PAPA
It's not Mr. Goldberg's fault. It's the free trade.

THE PHILOSOPHER
From a corner of the room.
What bitter bread!
[Com'è amaro questo pane!]
Enter Sam.

SAM
Who's the idiot who parked out front?

GIOVANNI
Why?

SAM
I might have known.
He signals toward the window. Through the window, we see an obese tow truck driver hook up Giovanni's station wagon. Seeing his station wagon being front-lifted, Giovanni rushes out of the Blue Bird.

EXT. BLUE BIRD CAFÉ. DAY.
The obese tow truck driver is about to pull out into busy St. Clair traffic. Giovanni is nearly run over in his attempt to stop him before he can pull away. The tow truck driver cavalierly rolls down his window, in response to Giovanni's frantic knocking.

GIOVANNI
What are you doing? There's still time left in the meter.

TOW TRUCK DRIVER
You see anyone else parked along here? Ever wonder how you got the spot?
The tow truck driver lifts his watch to the window.
It's past four, ding-dong. Check your watch.
Giovanni realizes the problem for the first time.

GIOVANNI
Look, I'll give you cash. Just put it down.

TOW TRUCK DRIVER
I've already called the sucker in. Best I can do is give you a
lift to the pound. Save you the cab.

GIOVANNI
Disgusted.
You choose this work? What kind of man chooses this work
that you do?

TOW TRUCK DRIVER
Bristling at the insult.
I'm being nice . . . offer him a lift. All I get is insults.

GIOVANNI
Put it down.

TOW TRUCK DRIVER
Let go of the truck.

GIOVANNI
You have to. I'm here.

TOW TRUCK DRIVER
Sing-songy.
Yeah? Maybe I do and maybe I don't and maybe you'll find
it wrapped around a pole. What's it going to be, Tony? You
want the lift or not?
Giovanni lets go of the door handle.

GIOVANNI
Contemptuously.
I pay the fine. I pay the cab. I don't ride with you.

TOW TRUCK DRIVER
Under his breath.
Fucking ingrate.
*Tow truck driver pulls out into the traffic, as Giovanni
flags down a cab.*

EXT. CAR POUND. LATE AFTERNOON. DARK.

*Pound is lit garishly with security lights and sur-
rounded by high, barbed-wire fencing. Mazilli's station
wagon pulls out of the gates to a chorus of hailstones
and barking German shepherds. He narrowly misses
the fat tow truck driver, who is pulling in with his next
prey in tow. The tow truck driver shows Mazilli his
middle finger.*

EST. EXT. MAZILLI AND LEONE HOMES. LATE AF-
TERNOON. DARK.

*Mazilli drives onto the street where he lives — a dense
street, where the owners park their cars curbside. It will
be immediately apparent from the exterior of Mazilli's
semi-detached house that it is unique on the block,
with eccentric embellishments — for example, an
ornate white iron gate which is really an antique
painted iron headboard.*

*The Mazilli house is attached to the house of his
in-laws, the Leones, with connected underground can-
tinas where Nonno Leone retreats periodically to listen
to the goings-on in his daughter's household through
an overturned glass pressed against a water pipe.*

*Nonno Leone is at the window when Giovanni arrives.
He watches his son-in-law's parking performance.
Giovanni's usual curbside spot has been taken by the
Volkswagen Rabbit of a neighbour, which hogs two
spots. Giovanni expertly backs the station wagon into
position, nudging the Volks into its place. Giovanni
gets out of the station wagon, slams the door and
approaches his house. He sees Nonno Leone at the
window. Nonno Leone lets the curtain drop. Giovanni
shakes his head, as if to say: "I can't deal with this
now," takes a deep breath, and enters his house.*

INT. MAZILLI HOME. EVENING.

It's a zoo: loud television music greets him. Giovanni pressed by the force of sound against the inside front door. Giovanni's point of view (p.o.v.): into the living-groom. Tony (his fourteen-year-old son) is on the phone, one blue-jeaned leg slung over the arm of the IKEA-style couch. He is staring at the T.V., one ear plugged into his Walkman, the other, into the phone.

TONY

To the phone.

So if we buy three tickets at eighteen bucks apiece and scalp them for forty a ticket, that's . . .

Tony punches numbers into his pocket calculator. Enter Diana (age seventeen) scantily clad for her Friday-night date, pulls the Walkman from Tony's free ear and answers the question before his calculator.

DIANA

A sixty-six dollar profit on a fifty-four dollar investment — one-hundred-and-twenty-two per cent. Where's my blow-dryer?

TONY

. . . Awesome.

DIANA

You've taken that blow-dryer again, you're burnt toast.

Seeing their father.

Oh, hi, Dad.

Diana plants a disarming kiss to his cheek as she spins around and heads back toward her bedroom.

TONY

Dad, can I borrow fifty-four bucks until tomorrow? Me and Gino have this terrific idea . . .

GIOVANNI

Not now, Tony.

TONY
But we have to line up by six o'clock tomorrow morning.
A hundred-and-twenty-two per cent profit.

GIOVANNI
I said not now.
*Giovanni's eldest son, Francesco, a romantic-looking
young man in his early twenties, enters frame, heading
toward the door.*

TONY
I'll split the take with you.

GIOVANNI
Where are you going? I need to talk to you.

FRANCESCO
It'll have to wait.
Seeing his father's disappointment.
Hey, Dad, it's Friday night.
*Francesco gives his father an affectionate pat on the
face and a complicitous male wink. Sound of car horn,
loudly honking. Diana reappears, grabs her coat and
runs for the door. Door slams. Giovanni goes to the
window and lifts the curtain. Red Camaro. Interior car
light briefly illuminates blond boyfriend, as Diana
opens passenger door and gets in.*

GIOVANNI
Who is this guy behind the horn?

INT. LEONE CANTINA. EVENING.
*Nonno Leone, in his "stethoscope" pose, takes a quick
glass of wine, turns the glass over and presses it to the
cantina wall.*

INT. MAZILLI KITCHEN. STILL LATER THAT NIGHT.
*The kitchen is modern black-and-white ceramic with
track lighting; copper pots hang from red IKEA wall*

units. Maria Mazilli, an attractive woman in her early forties, is massaging Giovanni's shoulders, attempting to comfort him. He sits at the table with his plate of pasta untouched.

MARIA

You want cheese? I'll grate you some cheese.

GIOVANNI

No cheese.

MARIA

Eat something. It'll make you feel better.

GIOVANNI

I can't eat.
      Maria sighs with concern, and kisses the crown of his head.

MARIA

It was a job. A job is not your real life anyway.

GIOVANNI

What is my real life?

MARIA

Me. Your family . . . We'll be O.K. You could retire tomorrow, if you wanted. There's plenty in the bank. You'll find another job.

GIOVANNI

It's not the job. I can get ten like it tomorrow.

MARIA

And you will. I know you.

GIOVANNI

No. Not like that. Never again. Maria, something died for me today.

MARIA

It's still fresh. Tomorrow, everything will look different. It always does.

GIOVANNI

No, you don't understand. Today, a door closed. A door closes in a man's face, he's a stranger. The years here made no difference at all.

MARIA

We'll go to bed. You'll wake up. We've got the wedding tomorrow. You love weddings.

GIOVANNI
Beat.
I'm not going.

MARIA

What do you mean you're not going? It's your godson. We've got to go.

GIOVANNI

I'm in no mood.

MARIA

You're giving the speech to the bride. It would be an insult.
Mazilli straightens. He turns and pounds his fist against the common kitchen wall that divides the Mazilli house from that of the Leones.

GIOVANNI
Loudly, winking to Maria.
Go to bed, old man. Your daughter's safe for tonight.
Maria smiles, thinking the worst is over.

INT. LEONE CANTINA. EVENING.
An offended Nonno Leone removes his ear from the glass and, filling the glass with wine, salutes the wall.

INT. LA ROTUNDA BANQUET HALL. LATE DAY.

*Close of wedding cake at head table. The camera pans
from the lowest tier up. On either side of the cake are
escalator-type stairs, mounted on the one side by ten
barbie-doll bridesmaids in blue, on the other by ten
Ken-doll ushers in blue tuxedos with black lapels. At
the apex of the cake are the bride and groom, sheltered
inside an illuminated glass bell topped with a blue bow
and doves. The plug that illuminates the glass bell also
operates a small fountain. Pull back to include head
table: the real bridesmaids and ushers dressed identi-
cally to the dolls on the cake.*

LA ROTUNDA BANQUET HALL. DANCE FLOOR.

*Francesco dances with his grandmother, Nonna Leone,
teasing the gaggle of adoring females who watch them.
Just off dance floor, Tony and his peers lean against the
wall in a darkened corner of the room, drinking beer,
laughing at their elders and speculating about the
sex-lives of their aunts.*

GINO

Can you imagine Zia Rosa doing it with Zio Rocco?

MIKE

How does he find it, with all that fat?

GINO

They must have a reinforced floor in their bedroom.

TONY

I'd give a day's pay to see them screw.

GINO

You wouldn't give a day's pay to see anything.

INT. LA ROTUNDA CLOAKROOM.

*Diana and her blond boyfriend neck ravenously be-
hind the coats.*

INT. LA ROTUNDA, JUST OFF DANCE FLOOR.
Scotch glasses and ashtrays litter a table, where the Bluebird Cronies play cards.

PAPA
If I go back, I go to Naples. Naples, that's my *terra d'amore*. I love better than my home town.

LUCIANO
What's in Naples?

GIOVANNI
What's here?

LUCIANO
You wouldn't say that, if you'd been back. At least we've all been back for a holiday. The first time I come back to Canada after a holiday, I kiss my house and I say, I never leave you again.

SONNY
Twenty years, make confuse.

LUCIANO
In my home town, if you fart, everybody smells it. Here, nobody knows your business.

PAPA
Nobody cares.

LUCIANO
Take the bathrooms, for sample.

PAPA
Again, with the bathrooms. He goes to Rome. Do we hear about the Coliseum? No, just the toilets.

LUCIANO
I like the toilets in Canada. You get used to see the crap disappear. One flush . . .

PAPA
. . . *Stupido,* it's the life, not the bathrooms.

LUCIANO
But the bathrooms are part of the life.
The Philosopher intones distantly, never quite part of the conversation.

THE PHILOSOPHER
You can't go home again; you must go home again. Home is the place you escape from; home is the place to which you escape.
[Non puoi tornare; devi tornare . . . La tua terra è da dove sei scappato; la tua terra è il tuo rifugio.]

GIOVANNI
There's nothing here for me anymore.

LUCIANO
Take it from me, a man of experience, there's nothing there, either.

PAN SHOT OF LONG SWEET TABLE.
An enormous blue-ice love boat melts on a platter at the centre of the sweet table. Off to one side of the sweet table, Nonno Leone, still dressed primly in his three-piece suit, snores loudly in his chair. Two children — a girl, bursting out of a pink-layered party dress, a little boy in dress-pants, vest and bow-tie — emerge from under the tablecloth and run off. Tony is collecting matches off the tables and stuffing them into his pockets. The camera following children, back to dance floor, where they weave in and about the dancing couples.

CRONIES. TABLE. LATER.
Maria comes to the table and pulls Giovanni to his feet, wanting to dance. Giovanni rises, staggering

slightly, adjusts himself, and escorts her cavalierly to the dance floor.

DANCE FLOOR. ANOTHER ANGLE. LATER.
Giovanni dances with Maria, ballroom style. He is a good dancer, and clearly enjoys weaving Maria around and about the dancing couples, who move to give them sway. This is a performance seen before, at other weddings. Giovanni, dancing, is a crowd pleaser. But he has had much more to drink than is his custom. He stumbles once, and when he speaks fervently into Maria's ear, he is sodden with sentimentality.

GIOVANNI
Remember our wedding, Maria?

MARIA
We danced so much, your feet hurt all the way to Canada, in those shoes your mother gave you.

GIOVANNI
You wore a white hat, with the feather. It blew off on the boat.

MARIA
That was the first time I saw a man cry.

GIOVANNI
So many first times.
[Quante prime volte.]
Giovanni kisses Maria. She blushes at this public display of affection, at their age in life.

GIOVANNI
It was a sign, Maria — that hat, those shoes . . . Have you forgiven me yet?

MARIA
For what?

GIOVANNI
I promised we'd return. Only one night, we were a couple in Italy.

MARIA
There's plenty of time, still.

GIOVANNI
No there's not. No time at all.
Giovanni is now dangerously close to tears.
Look at me.
He breaks step with the dance.
I'm free. For the second time in my life. Because I lost my job. Because my life is almost finished. Don't you see? It's a sign.
Luciano enters frame with Giovanni's drink. Protectively, Maria tries to intercept, but Luciano transfers the drink above her head and into Giovanni's hands before she can reach it. The music ends and the band leader announces:

BAND LEADER
Allora, the toast to the bride.

MARIA
Maybe you should let someone else . . .

GIOVANNI
No one else. It takes a free man to speak the truth.

LA ROTUNDA STAGE.
Scotch glass in hand, Giovanni careens toward the microphone. Reaching out for it, he trips on the chord. Flushed with dance and drink, he thinks he's delivering the speech of his life.

GIOVANNI
Little bride from Palermo, my godson met you last summer on his first trip to Italy. Stay in Abruzzi, I told him. *Ma, testa*

dura, he has to go south. What's in the south? Ah — *la bella Siciliana.*

> *The sound of general laughter. Giovanni's p.o.v.: close on bride. The bride appears bemused. Her face goes in and out of focus. One moment it is the face of the Sicilian bride, the next, the young Maria.*

Isn't she lovely. Pretending she understands.

> *General laughter. Voice drops, becoming an intimate duet with memory.*

This morning you made a promise in a language you began to learn only yesterday. Twenty-three years ago, I made a promise. It was on board the Michelangelo luxury liner. I was on my way to America with my bride —

ANGLE ON: MARIA. GIOVANNI'S P.O.V.:

> *His words turn the spotlight on a concerned Maria. She turns. Now sharply in, then out of focus, she is his young bride again.*

TONY

Not the Michelangelo boat story again.

DIANA

Version four-hundred and thirty-two.

> *Stage. Another angle.*

GIOVANNI

We were the immigrants, below deck, but we had eyes. We could still see. From Naples to New York, we watched the rich people dance . . .

DIANA

> *Groaning, voice over her father's.*

. . . in their gowns and tuxedos . . .

> *Stage. Another angle.*

GIOVANNI

I promised my bride: We will live again in Italy. We will be rich with our work from Canada. I will bring you back on the Michelangelo luxury liner — only we, Maria and Giovanni, will be the ones to dance.

Beginning to lose it.

I'm sorry, Maria.

Maria, as she makes her way through the wedding guests over to Francesco. She says something to him, as they both look, embarrassed, toward the stage. Near table: offside stage. Nonno Leone wakes up at the sound of his daughter's name. Seeing his son-in-law on the stage making a fool of himself, he scrambles toward the stage, in quest for the plug to pull on Giovanni:

NONNO LEONE

Are you farting with your brain?

[Hai il cervello che ti scorreggia?]

Stage. Another angle.

GIOVANNI

Francesco, four o'clock came at the factory, it used to kill me to think of you home from school; you'd have to let yourself in with the key you wore around your little neck. You don't want to hear anymore. Your father is like a record — a broken, Italian record. What's broken is my promise. And with it, this heart.

Francesco enters frame with determined steps, heading toward his father. Giovanni, aware that he must bring matters swiftly to a conclusion, raises his voice dramatically.

Bride from Palermo — go home while there's still time, while the promise is young!

Nonno Leone finds the plug. Francesco signals the band to begin playing.

BAND LEADER

E adesso tango.

The band starts playing — cha, cha, cha . . . as Giovanni is ushered off the stage by his son.

EXT. MAZILLI HOME. NIGHT.
Music of tango continuing. Family station wagon pulls up to curbside. Maria gets out of the back seat, and storms toward the house, as the rest of the family piles out. Giovanni staggers out of the passenger side, arms flailing as he rejects a hand from Francesco. He staggers over to the neighbour's Volkswagen Rabbit and relieves himself against the tire as Nonna Leone covers her eyes in scandalized modesty.

INT. MAZILLI KITCHEN. NIGHT.
Maria sets her purse and bomboniera down on the kitchen table. Giovanni enters and heads to the sink for water. Maria leaves kitchen without speaking to him.

INT. LEONE MASTER BEDROOM. NIGHT.
The Leone bed has a heavy dark wood headboard, its many feathered pillows covered with hand-embroidered white bed linens, obviously imported from Italy. As Nonna Leone struggles onto the high mattresses, Nonno Leone takes up his "stethoscope pose" at the wall, listening through his overturned wine glass.

INT. MAZILLI MASTER BEDROOM. NIGHT.
The Mazilli bed is modern. Giovanni lies prostrate in bed, looking ill; Maria is curled angrily on her side, her back to her husband.

MARIA
Angry.
Twenty-three years, we've never been back. Not even for a holiday! Not even for your mother's funeral! You won't go back, but it's all you talk about.

GIOVANNI
A day doesn't go by, I still don't think of her.
Maria is still on her own angry tangent.

MARIA

You said the ties with Italy were cut. You said it, not me!

GIOVANNI

She was the only one who, when I left, wished me well. "Don't worry about me," she said, "My love won't keep you here."

INT. LEONE BEDROOM. NIGHT.

NONNO LEONE

Che stupido, pazzo . . . Bananas, vitamins, the kids have everything here . . . he wants to go back to Italy. And for a woman!

INT. MAZILLI BEDROOM. NIGHT.

MARIA

Can't you see you're confused? Italy is finished. Why can't you just accept? There's nothing there for us anymore.
Giovanni pounds his chest and howls melodramatically.

GIOVANNI

Nothing is ever finished until it's finished in here. And in here, she's alive.

INT. LEONE BEDROOM. NIGHT.

NONNO LEONE

I feel sick.

NONNA LEONE

Put some *brioschi* in the glass. Listen to it fizz instead of walls, you'll digest better.

NONNO LEONE

You don't understand. Your son-in-law's in love with another woman. He's going back to Italy, for an old flame! [Una vecchia fiamma!]

INT. MAZILLI BEDROOM. NIGHT.

GIOVANNI
I'll tell you what's over. Canada is over.

MARIA
Listen, this plant closing has depressed you. It's only natural you have these thoughts.

GIOVANNI
No, you don't understand, it's not going to change. I'm not going to change. I've finally realized something.
Unable to comfort him, Maria takes him in her arms. They begin to make love — a hurt, needy love.

INT. LEONE BEDROOM. NIGHT.
Nonno Leone climbs back into bed.

NONNO LEONE
Veramente, I'm sick. *Portami all'ospedale.*

NONNA LEONE
Vecchio ubriacone, pretend you're dead until tomorrow morning. Then, if you're still sick, I'll take you to the hospital.

INT. MAZILLI BEDROOM. NIGHT.
A much calmer Giovanni and Maria cling to each other wordlessly. Maria strokes her husband's hair thoughtfully.

MARIA
You need a holiday. The new job can wait. Go to Italy. Finally. Go for a holiday. Go and see.

INT. MAZILLI MASTER BEDROOM. DAY.
Giovanni rummages frantically at the base of the clothes cupboard, searching for something. A suitcase lies open on the bed, half-packed with clothing.

FRANCESCO
Flipping his car keys.
C'mon, Dad. The agent said two hours before departure.
Tony lies on his parents' bed, placing his order.

TONY
Bring me back about twenty *Ciao, Roma* T-shirts, different
sizes . . . I'll screen *Ciao, St. Clair* on the back, sell them at
school . . .

FRANCESCO
I've put your Michelin guidebook in the outside pouch.

GIOVANNI
From inside the cupboard.
I don't need it. I find my own way, with my heart.

TONY
Still musing.
The CN Tower on one side, Coliseum on the other —
awesome.
*The Leones enter the bedroom. Nonna Leone hands a
brown paper bag to Maria.*

NONNA LEONE
He never had a stomach for strangers' food.

GIOVANNI
Still from inside the cupboard.
What strangers? I'm going home.

NONNO LEONE
Home is where your wife sleeps.
To Maria.
What's he doing travelling without you?

MARIA
Apologetically.
A holiday.

NONNO LEONE
Good husbands don't take holidays without their wives.
Watching his son-in-law's rummaging.
You think I don't know?

TONY
. . . Nah, scrap that order. Soccer T-shirts . . .

NONNO LEONE
. . . He's like his old man, the sailor.

GIOVANNI
From inside the cupboard.
My father had nothing to do with me. I raised myself.

NONNO LEONE
Roots don't wander too far from the stump, no matter how
hard they try.

NONNA LEONE
Whispering to her daughter.
You did right. Italy has always been Gina Lollobrigida for
him. *Ma,* Gina Lollobrigida is only Gina Lollobrigida up
there on the screen. *Non esiste.* Let him get close. He'll see
she has wrinkles and sagging boobs.
Close of Maria's face: uncertainty.

DIANA
Who's Gina Lollobrigida?

GIOVANNI
Ecco. Now I can go.
*He emerges from his search with an old pair of black
leather shoes. Fondly, he rubs the dust off the shoes,
and lays them in the suitcase on top of his clothes, soles
up. Tony picks up a shoe and examines it.*

TONY
You're taking these?

GIOVANNI

A gift from my mother. She bought these shoes with money she didn't have. I promised her someday I'd wear them back.

TONY

They're going to hurt.

GIOVANNI

A man should keep his promises, even if they hurt . . . especially if they hurt.

Decisively, Giovanni snaps shut the suitcase. He turns and seeks out Maria. He goes to her. Beat, as they look at each other. Giovanni locks her in his arms. Then he picks up the suitcase and heads out the door with Francesco.

EXT. ITALY, SPRING. MORNING.

Aerial travelling shot: A train is threading its way through a spectacular and sunlit countryside toward the coastal town of Vasto.

EST. TRAIN STATION. VASTO, ITALY. MORNING.

The train pulls into the station. A number of people disembark, met by family and friends. Then Giovanni emerges into the frame of the train doorway, looking dazed and disoriented. He squints at the dazzling sunlight with unaccustomed eyes. Giovanni is an oddity. He lugs a heavy suitcase and carry-on-bag, is dressed in Canadian tourist's clothing, but with the old Italian leather shoes. The first few steps Giovanni takes on the platform indicate he's in some kind of pain. He is hobbled by the shoes. He bends down to pick something out of a shoe. The bus into which the recent arrivals have loaded themselves, takes off in a cloud of dust and stones toward town. Giovanni misses it. When it passes, he emerges from the dust, straightening himself. He is thoroughly irritated at the moment's delay over a shoe that cost him the ride into town. Driving his cab like an extension of himself, the cabby (Antonio Tassista) pulls over to where Mazilli stands. He hops out, throws open the cab's trunk and grabs Giovanni's suitcases. Instinctively, Giovanni hangs on, and blurts out in English.

GIOVANNI

What are you doing?
They engage in a tug-of-war over the luggage.

CABBY

I help. You got somewhere to go? I take you.

GIOVANNI

I've arrived. I know where I am. I don't need your help.
The Cabby looks crestfallen, as if this is a personal affront:

CABBY

You going to walk from here?
Giovanni considers the hill, then his feet. Profiting from his indecision, the Cabby succeeds in extracting the suitcases from Giovanni and tosses them into his trunk.
Antonio Tassista at your service. You need something? A place to stay? I know everything there is to know.

GIOVANNI

Shoes.

CABBY

Shoes? This, too, we can arrange.
Cavalierly, he opens the cab door for Giovanni.

INT. CAB. MORNING.

GIOVANNI

So where did you learn English?

CABBY
In prison. By correspondence.

GIOVANNI
Nervously.
Yeah? What did you do?

CABBY
Me, nothing. They defamed me. They said I had . . . how
do you say? — *fatto il palo.*

GIOVANNI
Oh, you were the get-away man.

CABBY
These two guys wanted me to drive them to Chieti and wait.
A little later, they come out with a bag. They tell me to drive
fast. After, if they were so good to give me 500,000 lire,
why shouldn't I take it for that kind of service? There's no
law against gratuities.
*As the cab heads up the coastal hill into town, Mazilli
gazes at the surrounding sea and then the town. He
loves it. He doesn't know out of which window to look
first, as frisky as a child going on his first picnic in the
country. They mount the hill; the view opens.*

GIOVANNI
Halt!
*The Cabby slams on his breaks. Excitedly, Giovanni
scrambles out of the cab and out onto the meadow
overlooking the valley.*

EXT. HILL OVERLOOKING THE VALLEY. MORNING.
*Giovanni takes a deep breath and spins around, his
arms open.*

GIOVANNI
What a panorama. Finally, I can breathe again.

CABBY
Watching him from the cab, calls out.
So how long have you been holding your breath?

INT. CAB. MORNING.

GIOVANNI
Directing his driving.
No, not this way. Through the centre of town.
They enter the city limits.
Peep your horn, like it's a wedding.
Giovanni hangs out the window, waving and smiling like a passing dignitary. Local townspeople look up and watch the passing cab with curiosity. An old man, grinning toothlessly, waves back.

EXT. VASTO. TOWN CENTRE. DAY.
The taxi takes Giovanni to Vasto's downtown. It consists of a square, with a fountain, the town clock — the village monument. Fronting onto the square are merchant's shops. Giovanni gets out of the cab and hobbles over toward the fountain.

CABBY
The meter is running.

GIOVANNI
Let it run.
Giovanni takes off his shoes and socks and climbs into the fountain, sighing with satisfaction as his feet hit the cooling waters. He reaches down with his hands and baptises himself, splashing water over his face and head. Again, local reaction. Giovanni laughs and waves. Townspeople wave back indulgently, as if to say: "Crazy tourist, let him have his fun."

EXT. SHOE SHOP. DAY.
> *The Cabby pulls up behind a bus, across the square from the shoe shop. Mazilli's p.o.v.: close on store front:* DiPasquale Calzature.

GIOVANNI
I can't believe my eyes. It's still here.
> *A jubilant Giovanni steps out into the square, and is nearly run over in his wild excitement to make contact with the past.*

Wait for me.
> *The Cabby scrambles out of the cab after him.*

CABBY
I don't wait anymore.

INT DIPASQUALE CALZATURE. DAY.
> *Giovanni rushes in. An ancient DiPasquale, Sr. directs his son from an ornately carved oak chair. He holds a cane, which he wields like a cattle prod. The son, a harassed and hungry-looking character in his thirties, is balding with wisps of grey. They are in the midst of an argument.*

DIPASQUALE
I know why you want the keys. I have your number.
[So perchè vuoi le chiavi. So cosa stai combinando.]

THE SON
So why do I want the keys?
[E perchè mai vorrei le chiavi?]

DIPASQUALE
To lock me out.
[Così non posso più entrare.]

GIOVANNI
Excuse me . . .
[Scusate . . .]

36   DARLENE MADOTT

The Cabby touches the Son's shoulder in an attempt
to get his attention for Giovanni.

CABBY

Something comfortable. You sell running shoes?
[Delle scarpe comode. Vende scarpe da tennis?]

SON

Wait a minute. Can't you see my father and I are having a
discussion?
[Un momento, per favore. Non vedete che mio padre e io
stiamo discutendo.]

DIPASQUALE

You can't wait until I die.
[. . . Non puoi nemmeno aspettare fino a che sono morto.]

SON

You can't take it with you.
[Non puoi portare nulla nella tomba.]

DIPASQUALE

I knew it. All you want is my money.
 [Lo sapevo. Tutto ciò che vuoi sono i miei soldi!]
        DiPasquale struggles from his perch to pick up a shoe
        with the end of his cane in order to throw it at his son.
        Giovanni goes off on a tour of the store.

GIOVANNI
To Cabby.

I remember this store. It always had the best shoes. With a
store like this, a man could raise his family with honour . . .

CABBY

Such a waste . . .

DIPASQUALE

I have to die first.
[Devi aspettare che muoia.]

He gets the shoe on the end of his cane and lobs it at
the son. The son ducks; the Cabby catches it and blows
the dust off the shoe's black surface.

CABBY

If this were my business, I'd sell running shoes, not these
display shoes — shoes for funerals . . .
The son shrieks hysterically, as a second shoe hits him.

SON

This shop is my grave.
[Questo negozio sarà la mia tomba.]

CABBY

. . . No repeat business, unless you plan to die twice.
He laughs at his own joke.

DIPASQUALE

Just as hysterical, lobbing a third shoe:
Tomb, is it? Then, I'll sell your tomb.
[Una tomba? Se è una tomba, allora la vendo la tua tomba.]

SON

Laughing hysterically.
What makes you think you could sell it? Who'd buy this
piece of antiquity?
[Cosa ti fa pensare che lo puoi venderlo. A chi può intessare
questo pezzo di vecchiume?]
In his own world, Giovanni runs his hand reverently
along the shelves.

GIOVANNI

My mother could never afford. Now her son can afford!

DIPASQUALE

You couldn't sell if your life depended on it.
[Non potresti vendere néanche a un bambino.]
Determinedly, the old man rises to his feet and grabs
Giovanni's arm, as if for balance. Unexpectedly, he
reaches into his pocket and pulls out a set of keys,

dangling them in front of Giovanni at the same time as he casts a malevolent glance back at the son.

DIPASQUALE
To Giovanni.
You want to control your own life, you need your own keys. With your own keys, nobody controls you. Not even a son. [Se voi volete essere in controllo della vostra vita, dovete avere le chiavi del vostro negozio e nessuno ve le può portare via. Nemmeno un figlio.]
He drops the keys into Giovanni's palm, still clinging to his wrist. Beat, as Giovanni stares at the keys, incredulous.
DiPasquale's eyes twinkle.
You want the keys, they're yours. Naturally at the right price.
[Se vuoi le chiavi sono tue. Naturalmente al prezzo giusto.]

GIOVANNI
Impulsively.
How much?
[Quanto volete?]

SON
To his father.
. . . Sei pazzo?

CABBY
Simultaneously, to Giovanni.
. . . Are you crazy?

EXT. MAZILLI'S STREET. CANADA. NIGHT.
Snow tumbles in front of car headlights; Diana and boyfriend park up the street where the Mazillis live, get out of the car and rush, huddled, along the snow-embanked sidewalk.

EXT. MAZILLI HOME. NIGHT.

Their breath steaming in the cold night air, Diana and her boyfriend neck ravenously as she fumbles with the key to the basement door at the back of the house.

INT. CANTINA. NIGHT.

Diana and her boyfriend enter the house and throw themselves against a sack of potatoes in the cantina. They leave their coats on. It's as cold in the cantina as outside. Diana is nervous of being discovered. Her tension almost outweighs her pleasure, and the boyfriend becomes ever more impatient with her as her fears and hands check his every advance.

INT. LEONE CANTINA. NIGHT.

Insomniac old Nonno Leone is seeking his nightly comfort in the adjoining cantina when he overhears his granddaughter's adolescent fumbles. His whiskery old eyebrows go up in alarm. Split screen: Quickly quaffing his wine, Nonno Leone turns his glass over and places it against the wall, directly parallel to the potato sack on the other side. The sighs of pleasure are unmistakable. Nonno Leone goes to a bread box in his basement, where he keeps an extension phone, just in case of burglars elsewhere in the house, lifts the lid and pulls out an old black receiver. He dials his daughter's number.

INT. MAZILLI MASTER BEDROOM. NIGHT.

Maria answers the phone from her bed, and hears her father's voice like the voice of doom.

NONNO LEONE

My daughter sleeps, while things are happening beneath her very bed.

MARIA

What's it now, Pa.

NONNO LEONE
Ominously.
In the cantina. Your daughter . . . with a man.
Click of phone being returned to receiver. Maria throws on a housecoat and heads down the stairs.

INT. MAZILLI BASEMENT. NIGHT.
Diana hears the footsteps overhead and manages to get the boyfriend out the basement door while she hastily buttons herself. Her mother pulls the chord of an overhead light bulb and the basement fills with light. There stands Diana, her face chapped red from the stubbled caresses of her boyfriend.

MARIA
Gently reproachful.
Is this how you prepare for the math competition — counting kisses?

INT. MAZILLI KITCHEN. NIGHT.
Maria fixes her daughter a large bun sandwich with salami and mortadella, and fills a glass of milk. While her daughter eats with the appetite of youth, Maria sits across from her and watches.

MARIA
Men want what they can't have. If you give it to them too easily, the meal is eaten, the appetite gone. This young man, if you really want him, keep him hungry.
A bleary-eyed Tony comes into the kitchen in his pyjamas.

TONY
What's up?

MARIA
Sit down, I'll make you a sandwich.

Nonno Leone arrives in his housecoat and slippers,
bearing a bottle of wine in one hand, prosciutto in the
other. To Nonno Leone.
It was just the kids. They were hungry.
Nonno Leone sits down at the table. Maria makes him
a sandwich too. Francesco enters. He heads straight for
the kitchen sink where he fills himself a huge glass of
water. Everyone watches, as he downs it thirstily.

NONNO LEONE
Back in Italy, I had a dog used to come home just to drink.
I could always tell he'd had a good night by the level of
water in the bowl.
The old man laughs rakishly.
Adding soberly.
Daughters don't come through cantina doors, when fathers
stay home.

MARIA
Pa, one more word against my family, you leave this table
for good.
Nonno Leone blinks, then bites sullenly into his sand-
wich.

DIANA
Is that why you let Dad go to Italy? So he'd lose his appetite?
Maria smiles and gives her daughter a complicitous
wink.

EXT. ITALY: OUTDOOR OSTERIA, OVERLOOKING
SEA. NIGHT.
Giovanni and the Cabby sit outdoors under the pink
canopy of the Osteria California, devouring a fabulous
entrée of seafood and fettucini out of great, steaming
bowls.

GIOVANNI
Eyes closed.

La migliore zuppa di pesce. I want to eat like this every day, for the rest of my life. To eat with the smell of the sea. *L'odore del mare mi calmerà.*

> *The white linen tablecloths flap in the sultry evening sea breeze, blowing up from the ocean. Suddenly, the chinese lanterns encircling the patio come on at the same time as the town lights illuminate in the distance. The synchronicity is magical. Collective sigh, then sprinkling of spontaneous applause, as the diners appreciate the poetry of the night. Suddenly, the peace is broken by the loud voice of the Vigile, who sits at another table of the Osteria.*

VIGILE
This pasta is overcooked.
[Questa pasta è scotta.]

WAITRESS
I didn't make it.
[Non l'ho fatta io.]

VIGILE
That's no excuse. Even a blind man can see it's a dish of glue.
[Che razza di discorso è. Anche un cieco può vedere che è colla.]

GIOVANNI
To the cabby.
Who is this guy?
> *The Cabby two-facedly salutes the Vigile with his glass of wine and smiles.*

CABBY
Quietly, to Giovanni.
The Vigile. A real pain in the ass. But it's O.K. Here in Vasto, we're like one big family. *Un circolo.* We go round and round. Every day, the same faces. Ignore him, our Vigile. Eat, enjoy your meal.

The proprietor refreshes their wine.

PROPRIETOR

Sure, it's O.K. to be so particular, especially when you don't pay. He doesn't pay and complains . . .

[Fa pure il difficile e pensare che non paga néanche un centesimo . . .]

> *The waitress, near tears, attempts to take the plate away, but the Vigile has not finished with her yet.*

VIGILE

Taste it if you don't believe me. I want to see if you can swallow.

[Assaggiala, se non mi credi. Voglio vedere se riesci a mandarla giù!]

> *The Vigile addresses the Osteria, at large.*

Every night, I'm disbelieved.

[Tutte le sere la stessa storia.]

GIOVANNI

You mean you perform here every night? It's no wonder you dine alone. It must be your wife who books your performances.

[Mi volete dire che recitate qui tutte le sere. Per forza mangiate da solo. Scommetto che vostra moglie vi fa da impresario.]

> *Giovanni laughs alone. The proprietor and regular patrons exchange meaningful glances. Giovanni has definitely stepped on touchy toes.*

VIGILE

Someone asked you?

[Ma chi ti ha chiesto niente?]

MAITRE D'

We'll bring you the specialty, compliments of the house.

[Ecco un piatto speciale, omaggio della padrona.]

GIOVANNI
Enjoy your free food. Your quarrel is with yourself. Not the
girl or the pasta.
[Godetevi il cibo gratis fino a che potete. Siete arrabbiato
con voi stesso, non con la ragazza o la pasta.]

VIGILE
You want to wear this pasta, you like it so much?
[Vuoi mangiarla tu visto che ti piace tanto?]

*Vigile stands imperiously, holding the plate of pasta.
The proprietor rescues it deftly out of his hands. The
Cabby snaps his finger and the restaurant mandolin
player tosses him the guitar. The Cabby interposes
himself between Giovanni and Vigile, and strums the
first chords of a lively tarantella. He engages the whole
restaurant and thus defuses the situation.*

EXT. OSTERIA. MUCH LATER SAME NIGHT.
*The restaurant is all but deserted. The Cabby Sings
now in a quieter mode — Santa Lucia Luntana — a
song about a man who leaves Naples to make it rich
elsewhere. But when the moon rises over his strange
city, the man realizes he has money: He doesn't have
Naples. Giovanni has an arm around the Cabby's
shoulder, his free arm raised in song with the Cabby.
Wiping his eyes on the osteria linen.*

GIOVANNI
This is the music I recognize . . . I'm so happy. *Così felice.*

EXT. MAZILLI HOME. MARCH AFTERNOON.
*Music of "Santa Lucia" continuing. A cab pulls up with
Giovanni inside, bearing suitcases and gifts. Giovanni
rushes into the house, anxious to discharge his burden.*

INT. MAZILLI KITCHEN. AFTERNOON.
The table is set, the evening meal about to begin. Everyone is assembled, including the Leones. Giovanni bursts onto the scene.

NONNO LEONE
Back so soon?
Hopeful.
You didn't like Italy?

GIOVANNI
Italy was wonderful, wonderful.
Excitedly, Giovanni takes his presents from the boxes and bags, and thrusts them upon the family — T-shirts for Tony, embossed with americanisms:
Everyone speaks English over there now.
He gives a white, silk nightgown to Maria.
The mimosa were in bloom, Maria. You should have smelt the air, it was wonderful, wonderful.
He presents a silver wine-tasting cup to Nonno Leone. Lifting the cup to his ear.
A better conductor than glass.
A gift, a comment for everyone. Everyone is pleased with their gift, even Nonno. Amidst the tissue paper and commotion, Giovanni announces quietly:
I bought a shoe store. We're going home.
At first, it doesn't register. Maria is still fondling her nightgown. Slowly, the meaning of what he has just said breaks in upon her. She looks at him.

MARIA
What did you say?

GIOVANNI
We're going home. To Italy.
Close of Maria's face: The smile fades. Confusion. Then, incredulity.

FRANCESCO
Are you in reverse, or what? It's the kids who leave home, not their parents.

GIOVANNI
Leaving home? Who said anything about leaving home. You're all coming with me.

DIANA
Count me out. Len and I are getting married . . .

GIOVANNI
. . . Len, who? You mean this guy behind the car horn? You think I'm going to let you waste your brains on some Len? You'll marry when I say so.
> *Diana flees to her bedroom. Her sobs can be heard into the kitchen, where the chaos continues.*
That's one less problem we'll have to worry about over there.

TONY
What's a dollar worth in lire?

NONNA LEONE
> *Starts to cry.*
I no wunderstan.

NONNO LEONE
Don't cry, old woman, we go nowhere. Canada is our grave!
> *Nonna Leone cries even harder.*

GIOVANNI
You'll love it over there. We'll be a family again. You'll see how happy we'll all be.
> *Through the silence, we hear Diana and Nonna Leone weeping. Throughout it all Maria is silent. Giovanni keeps his eyes trained on her, trying to get some reading from her. Her face is closed.*

FRANCESCO
To his mother.
Are you going to let him do this to us? To you?
Losing patience, Giovanni announces before he storms out:

GIOVANNI
In a family, the father decides; the mother follows. I've decided. There'll be no more talk.
[Il padre decide; le moglie deve seguire.]
Close of Maria. Giovanni's pronouncement ignites anger in her eyes.

INT. MAZILLI MASTER BEDROOM. DAY.
Maria sits cross-legged at the foot of their bed, a glass of wine on the carpet beside her, eyes closed, her jaw set. Enter Giovanni. Quietly, he sits beside her. He tries to put an arm around her shoulders. She shrugs him off and moves to another part of their room. His voice follows her.

GIOVANNI
Maria, never in a hundred years will we belong here.

MARIA
Twenty-three years, we've lived here. We had our kids here. Our life is here!

GIOVANNI
I can't live here anymore.

MARIA
Then you can't live anywhere.

GIOVANNI
Then I can't live anywhere.
Maria turns and faces him. She studies his face. Giovanni stares back at her.

MARIA
Oh my God.

GIOVANNI
What?

MARIA
What? What you're going to do. What you've already done!

GIOVANNI
Maria, I was home. I was myself again.

MARIA
It wasn't bad enough we had to be immigrants here? You want our kids to be immigrants over there?

GIOVANNI
They'll know Italy the moment they step off the plane. They have our blood, Maria.

MARIA
I can't believe you are doing this — *ancora!*

GIOVANNI
I love you, Maria.

MARIA
Twenty-three years ago, you did this to me.

GIOVANNI
It was the best mistake we ever made.

MARIA
But to make it again!

GIOVANNI
Where's my co-adventurer? Where's the gypsy girl I married?

MARIA
She grew up. She settled down. In Canada!

GIOVANNI
We had the courage, once, Maria. Did our courage take us only this far?

MARIA
And if we go back, how far will we have gone?

GIOVANNI
We had the courage to want only ourselves.

MARIA
That you could make such a choice — without me.

GIOVANNI
Talking quickly, searching for the right spot.
Twenty-three years ago you made a choice. You remember our picnic in the country? You and me and the butcher's son — your father's choice. You cut your hand. He left us alone to get you some water from the river . . . I licked your blood.
Giovanni clasps her hand and holds it dramatically to his heart. He looks imploringly into her eyes. With passion.
I licked your blood, Maria . . . I am still the Giovanni you chose. You are still the Maria who chose me.

EXT. MAZILLI HOME. DAY.
A determined and impervious Mazilli stands outside his home with a fat St. Clair real estate agent. The agent puts his foot on the fender of his status car, his fat knee supporting the For Sale sign which Mazilli uses as a clip-board to pen his signature to the listing agreement. Nonno Leone, from his front porch, shouts imprecations at his son-in-law.

NONNO LEONE
You think I'll follow you like the last time, just so you can't rob me a second time. Now you steal my daughter and her kids. You've killed me twice!

*Nonna Leone joins them on the verandah. A handker-
chief to her face, she plucks at the sleeve of her
husband, trying to make him come inside. Above the
excited rantings of Nonno Leone, we hear the ham-
mer, as the agent begins pounding a for-sale sign into
Mazilli's front lawn.*

My daughter's happy here. Even you. You're happy here.
What happened?

GIOVANNI
Don't you understand, old man? It wasn't enough. It wasn't
home.

NONNO
Home?
Under his breath.
What is this fantasy — home?
[Che cosa è questa fantasia?]
To Giovanni.
Everyone from there is here. What do you think you're
going to find there? Ghosts?
*Francesco comes out of the Leone house. He brushes
past them both, gets into his red Camaro, and drives
off. Like the voice of doom.*
Sons have their own wills, Giovanni, sometimes as strong
as their father's. He'll leave you, anyway. You think Italy
can stop him?
*The Real Estate Agent points toward the verandah
where Nonno Leone stands.*

REAL ESTATE AGENT
To Giovanni.
Is that house for sale, too?

NONNO LEONE
Hysterically.
You want to sell something. Sell me six feet of the *cimitero*.
Canada is my grave!

NONNA LEONE
Her voice a wail.
My daughter married a man as stubborn as her father.
[Mia figlia ha sposato un uomo testardo, come suo padre.]

MR. SPADAFORA'S AUTOBODY SHOP. DAY.
*Mr. Spadafora greets Giovanni as he enters the garage,
wordlessly signals with his eyes over to where
Francesco is working, his head beneath the hood of a
car. Giovanni goes over and stands awkwardly beside
his son, waiting for Francesco to look up and acknow-
ledge his presence, his hands idle at his sides. He stuffs
them in his pockets, looking ill-at-ease. Mr. Spadafora
sits at a desk in the office off the autobody shop, doing
his monthly bills, trying to disappear.*

GIOVANNI
I look at you, I see myself.
*Francesco is silent as he turns the wrench angrily and
hurls it into the tool box. Then he takes out another.*
I want you to play a little before you make a choice, to make
love to your life.

FRANCESCO
What about what I want? Have you thought about that?
*Francesco buries his head back under the hood.
Giovanni lowers his voice to almost a whisper.*

GIOVANNI
You want to spend all your life turning bolts under cars for
Mr. Spadafora?
Mr. Spadafora puts his eyes back in the bills.

FRANCESCO
You do any better for Mr. Goldberg?

GIOVANNI
No. But I will. We will. You with me.

*Francesco throws himself onto the dory and pulls
himself under the body of the car, out of sight of his
father.*
Giovanni grows excited. Loudly.
You could become an engineer — a real engineer, an Italian
engineer. What country gave birth to Marco Polo, Christo-
pher Columbus? It was Italians who built the first roads . . .
*Francesco is silent. Giovanni stares down at his son's
workboots.*

INT. MAZILLI KITCHEN. DAY.
*Two shot: Francesco and Maria. In a rare moment of
intimacy, Francesco seeks his mother alone. She is in
the kitchen, cutting a chicken at the sink. Francesco
thinks he'll find a sympathetic ear in her. To his
surprise, he finds his mother takes her husband's part.*

FRANCESCO
Why? Is he *pazzo?*

MARIA
Don't call him that. You never call him that.

FRANCESCO
Even you? A few weeks ago you weren't talking. Now he's
turned even your head? Has everyone gone crazy?
*Francesco starts to leave. Impulsively, Maria takes his
hand and makes him sit down with her at the kitchen
table.*

MARIA
The night you were born, your father and I were in Canada
little more than a year. I missed the dinner at the hospital.
When the nurse comes in, I don't know how to tell her I
need to eat. Please, I say, and I show her my mouth with
my hand. I feel so stupid. She tells me the kitchen is closed,
but she'll find something for me. All night, I wait. I'm so
alone, that night, so alone. And I think, this is all the fault
of Canada. I miss my mother, I miss my language. But

somehow, I get used to it. I even grow to love Canada. I learn my home is wherever my husband and children are. Francesco, a mother has a child. She gives it life, and asks nothing in return. I promise, I will ask only one thing of you, only this once. Come with us. If you won't do it for him, do it for me.

Francesco is unspeakably moved by his mother's words. Beat, as they gaze at each other. Francesco shoves away from the table and leaves the room before she can see his tears.

INT. THE BLUE BIRD CAFÉ. DAY.
Giovanni, full of the pride of his imminent announcement, goads his cronies.

GIOVANNI
It's a natural law. You gotta die where you born.

SONNY
But what if your wife's French, your kids Canadian, and you're Italian?

LUCIANO
Mocking Giovanni.
It's a natural law, the man's Italian, they all gotta die in Italy.

PAPA
I gave my lawyer $10,000 to bury me in Italy.

LUCIANO
I know your lawyer, he'll pocket the money and bury you here.

PAPA
I'll sue the bastard.

LUCIANO
Ciucciolone, how are you going to sue if you're dead?
Papa hesitates, and then brushes Luciano aside as if this is a minor detail.

PAPA
I find a way.

GIOVANNI
Here it is. My way. This time, for real!
*Giovanni takes the agreement of purchase and sale out
of his breast pocket and tables it. Stunned silence.*

PAPA
What you talk about?

GIOVANNI
The house — I sold it.

LUCIANO
No shit!
*The cronies descend on the paper with a devouring
curiosity.*

THE PHILOSOPHER
I have lost my home, my country, my heart. I am an
immigrant.
[Io ho perso casa, patria, e cuore. Sono un emigrante!]

LUCIANO
Keep the noise down. Can't you see we're trying to con-
centrate?

PAPA
You did well.
[Hai venduto bene.]

GIOVANNI
Proud of himself.
Of course. I drive a hard bargain.

PAPA
And the store in Italy? How much did it cost?
[Quanto l'hai pagato?]

GIOVANNI
Don't worry. There's enough left over to put free shoes on everyone in Vasto.

SONNY
So sudden.

GIOVANNI
Hey, it takes twenty-three years to think about, and one moment to decide.

LUCIANO
You can leave us behind? Just like that?

GIOVANNI
The door is always open. You visit me there, anytime. Mazilli's Shoes. Ask anyone in Vasto. Within a month, they'll all know me.
> *Jubilant, Mazilli leaps onto his chair. From atop this perch, he breaks into a famous song from the Abruzzi region.*

Vola, vola, vola . . .
> *One by one, his cronies, then the whole Blue Bird cafe, joins in, until everyone is singing. Luciano finds himself weeping in mid-song. His nostalgic sobs can be heard comically above the voices of the rest. Giovanni leaps from his chair, kisses the sobbing Luciano.*

LUCIANO
Don't leave me here.
[Non lasciarmi qua.]
> *Still singing, Giovanni dances to the door, claps money on the counter beside the cash, turns back once toward them all, and waves mockingly.*

EST. ITALY. DAY.
> *Aerial travelling shot. Cab. Its rooftop laden with luggage, the cab threads its way through the country-side toward the coastal town of Vasto in a torrential*

downpour. The cab pulls to a halt in front of the store, formerly DiPasquale Calzature, now heavily boarded. Rain pours off adjoining rooftops and into the gutters. The boarded shop looks mean and depressing.

INT. CAB. DAY.

Wedged between the Cabby and Maria, Mazilli throws his arm behind the neck rest and faces the back seat with a broad grin.

GIOVANNI

Ecco: Mazilli Calzature.

DIANA

You've got to be joking.

FRANCESCO

This is it?

TONY

It looks better from the inside, right?

Tony puts his finger down his throat, as if to barf.

EXT. STORE. DAY.

The Mazilli family and Cabby make a dash for it in the rain, holding sweaters and jackets over their heads. Giovanni fumbles at the door with an ancient key.

INT. SHOE STORE. DAY.

It is pitch dark. Then, grey light illuminates Giovanni's eager face as he and Francesco pry the board from a window. Their eyes follow the light back into the room. It is a dusty, depressing shambles.

FRANCESCO

Christ, Dad, were you blindfolded?

GIOVANNI

You've got to see beyond walls. A little fresh paint . . .

Maria walks into the shaft of light, her purse and luggage still in hand. Plaster breaks away from the ceiling and crumbles to the floor. She looks up at the wet patch on the ceiling from which the plaster fell.

CABBY
Your father is a man of vision.
Giovanni steps over the plaster, undaunted.

GIOVANNI
This is where the Bruno Magli collection will go.

CABBY
Running shoes over here, near the door.

TONY
Yeah — Michael Jordan.

GIOVANNI
No running shoes. Only the best Italian leather.

INT. APARTMENT ABOVE MAZILLI'S SHOES. DAY.
Diana opens a cupboard. A mouse scampers out. She closes the door quickly.

DIANA
It's a bad dream. Somebody pinch me.
She squeals and whips around quickly. The Cabby, winking, has obviously obliged. Francesco opens the shutters out onto a dripping back courtyard. Sound of rain echoing against stone.

FRANCESCO
With irony.
Charming.
Maria opens a door and is confronted with an ancient cupboard-sized bathroom. She pulls a chord and watches the toilet flush noisily; the yellowed water descends and new water raises in the bowl, leaving the stain untouched. Close on Maria: despair. Giovanni

*appears in the door frame behind her. Maria adjusts
her face. Sensitive to his audience, Giovanni tries to
engage Maria in a waltz toward the centre of the
apartment. Maria gives in briefly to this performance
before their children. The Cabby begins singing and
tries to dance with Diana, who petulantly rejects his
advance. Maria concludes the dance and rolls up her
sleeves. It is the signal to her family to begin work. As
she takes control of the ship, she marches past the
Cabby and says to him icily:*

MARIA
You were with him, that day?

INT. MAZILLI APARTMENT. DAY.
*Francesco and Tony, wearing only blue jeans, stripped
to the waist, whitewash walls. Francesco steps back to
look admiringly at his work. Tony gives him a pat on
the back with his brush, leaving a patch of white paint
on a muscular shoulder-blade. Giovanni plasters the
ceiling, completely absorbed by the work. He finishes
off the job with a proud, creative twirl. Diana dunks
a rag into a bucket of water, rebelliously hits the floor
with the rag and begins scrubbing. Maria washes a
window. She looks beyond into the courtyard to where
a neighbour, watching her, hangs out her laundry.
Maria waves to the neighbour. The neighbour smiles
and waves back.*

EXT. MAZILLI'S SHOES. SUMMER. DAY.
*All energy, Giovanni is displaying shoes inside a now
glistening shop window. Like a goldfish in a bowl, he
is being watched from without by a gaggle of old men
at a table in the square.*

INT. MAZILLI'S SHOES. DAY.

The Mazilli children descend into the shop from the apartment overhead. From his fishbowl, Giovanni waves them off encouragingly.

GIOVANNI

Enough work for now. Go, explore. Bring me back the stories of your adventures.

As they leave store.

DIANA

Muttering.

At least someone's happy.

TONY

It's a performance. Reality hasn't sunk in yet.

FRANCESCO

Keep your thoughts to yourselves. They have enough to worry about, without us.

EXT. STREET IN VASTO. DAY.

The three Mazilli children walk through town, turning heads, with their talk in English. Close of their retreating backsides: Diana, hips swaying; Tony, hands in pockets, kicking a coke can across echoing cobblestones; Francesco, beginning to look around with curiosity.

EXT. MAZILLI'S SHOES. DAY.

His backside to the camera, the uniformed Vigile (the same Vigile we saw earlier at the seaside restaurant) watches the shoe store, his hands behind his back, arrogantly rocking up and down on the points of his shoes. He turns. Close on face that is to become so insidious a presence for Giovanni.

EXT. MAZILLI'S SHOES. DAY.
> *Now in civilian clothes, the Vigile comes up to the shop. He has his two bratty children in tow. They enter the shop.*

INT. MAZILLI'S SHOES. DAY.
> *The Vigile's kids are busy in the shop, touching and turning over everything, as if they own the place. Maria fusses after them in a flustered way, reducing to order the chaos they leave in their spoiled wakes. Giovanni casts a worried glance in their directions.*

THE VIGILE
I need shoes for the kids. I just bought shoes a month ago, from DiPasquale. You know how it is, they grow so fast.
[Mi servono delle scarpe per i miei bambini. Le ho comperate un mese fa da DiPasquale, ma sono già diventate strette.]

GIOVANNI
Delighted to have a customer.
Take your time, look around.
[Fate pure con comodo.]

THE VIGILE
You don't know who I am?
[Ma lei sa chi sono io?]

GIOVANNI
No, who are you?
[No. Chi è lei?]

THE VIGILE
I pass by every morning.
[Passo di quà tutte le mattine.]

GIOVANNI
Oh, you're the policeman.
[Oh, siete un poliziotto.]

THE VIGILE

That's right, that's right. Very good.

[Bravo, proprio così.]

> *The kids, who have been trying on shoes, make their*
> *selections. It comes time to pay. Maria goes behind the*
> *cash register and smiles at the man with an expectant*
> *face. But the Vigile is reluctant with his wallet.*

It's too bad, there's no parking around here. By the way,
I've noticed you put a little table outside with the shoes on
display.

[Peccato che non c'è parcheggio qui intorno. A proposito
ho notato che avete messo un banchetto sul marciapiede.]

GIOVANNI

The tourists love it.

[Sì, è per i turisti.]

THE VIGILE

You have a licence for this?)

[Ce l'avete il permesso?]

> *Giovanni doesn't understand. Maria picks it up right*
> *away. She is wrapping up the shoe boxes, all ready to*
> *give them to the Vigile. They are on the same wave*
> *length.*

MARIA

Maybe we should give him the shoes. Customer relations . . .

> *Giovanni, catching on finally, places a nervous hand*
> *firmly on the boxes and scribbles out the bill, handing*
> *it to the Vigile, who looks at the bill with disapproval.*

THE VIGILE

You gave me a discount. Fifteen percent. Why?

[Perchè mi avete fatto lo sconto? Quindici per cento.]

GIOVANNI

Because you were a good customer of DiPasquale.

[Perchè eravate un buon cliente di DiPasquale.]

The Vigile pays the bill, grabs his kids' hands, and leaves the shop in a huff. Giovanni and Maria exchange glances, the same thought in their eyes — this man means trouble.

No more discounts, not even for the Mayor. I will pay my taxes. I will run my business. Next week, the salesman from Milano is coming. Mazilli's Shoes will be the exclusive vendor of Milano shoes in Vasto. To hell with the table outside. We don't need a table. No, leave the table. If the law exists, it exists for me too. I'll make an application for the licence. No discounts. Not even for the Mayor.

INT. CITY HALL. DAY.
Mazilli stands in a long line-up outside a wicket. He gets to the wicket.

GIOVANNI
I want to make application for a permit.
[Vorrei richiedere una licenza.]
Without looking up, the Functionary hands him a piece of paper. Mazilli takes it to a nearby chair and fills it out laboriously. He then takes it back to the Functionary behind the wicket who, without looking up, slides it under a huge pile of papers.

EXT. MAZILLI'S SHOES. DAY.
The local sign painter has just hung a sign from Giovanni's shoe shop, which extends out into the street: Mazilli Calzature. Giovanni appraises the sign proudly. No sooner does he finish paying the sign painter, when the Vigile approaches, this time in uniform, his head shaking, pencil and ticket pad in hand, pointing with the rubber end to the sign.

THE VIGILE
You have a permit?
[Avete una licenza per l'insegna?]

GIOVANNI

Did DiPasquale have a permit? I'm just replacing what was
there.

[Sto solo rimpiazzando l'insegna di DiPasquale.]

> *Without answering his question, the Vigile rips off a
> large yellow ticket and gives it to Giovanni.*

I have a business to run . . .

[Devo fare i miei interessi.]

INT. MAZILI'S SHOES. DAY.

> *Giovanni places the large yellow ticket in a drawer
> behind the cash.*

EXT. MAZILLI'S SHOES. EARLY MORNING.

> *Giovanni stands just off the street outside his shop,
> handing out flyers announcing a sale. He greets each
> townsperson with a good morning smile as he places
> a flyer in their hand. Once behind him, the local
> townspeople typically glance at the flyer and throw it
> away. The Vigile approaches Giovanni, whose smile
> disappears when he recognizes him.*

THE VIGILE

They do this in America, pollute the streets? Do you have
a permit?

[Fanno così in America? Buttano la roba per le strade? Ce
l'avete la licenza?]

> *The Vigile has his trusty pencil and ticket pad in hand,
> points the rubber end at the litter fluttering down main
> street behind Giovanni.*

GIOVANNI

For this I need a permit?

[Non ditemi che ho bisogno di una licenza speciale per
distribuire dei volantini!]

THE VIGILE

So many new ideas. You should ask me first about these new ideas.

[Avete così tante idee per la testa, che sarebbe meglio che le discuteste con me prima.]

> *The Vigile rips off another large yellow ticket and stuffs it into Giovanni's breast pocket with a mean little smirk. He leaves. The Cabby, who has witnessed everything, approaches Giovanni and plucks the ticket from his pocket, giving him a consoling pat to the shoulder.*

CABBY

Appeal it.

GIOVANNI

Appeal?

CABBY

Of course. In Italy, people die before their appeals can be heard.

GIOVANNI

What's the point of that?

CABBY

Stupido. That is the point.

INT. MAZILLI'S SHOES. MORNING.

> *In one glance, Maria takes in the ticket, Giovanni, and the Cabby, of whom she clearly disapproves.*

MARIA

> *Ambiguous, whether she means the ticket, or the Cabby.*

Ancora?

> *Giovanni hands her the yellow ticket, which she adds to the growing pile. The Cabby bows to Maria respectfully, and says to Giovanni in parting:*

CABBY
Don't wait too long.

EXT. VASTO'S MAIN SQUARE. EVENING.
It is the hour of the passeggiata. Tony, Diana and Francesco sit at the table of a Gelateria, just off the central square, having ice cream. At the table beside them is a mixed group of young men and women. The Mazilli children seem clearly to be enjoying the spectacle of young and old walking by, displayed in all their finery, the exercise of watching and being watched.

TONY
Appreciatively
It's like a parade.

DIANA
Affecting a sophistication, she hasn't yet achieved.
How quaint the local customs.

FRANCESCO
Mom and Dad should come out. This must be one of the things they missed.

DIANA
They're always working. I don't remember them working this hard in Canada.

FRANCESCO
You just didn't see it.
Angela walks by. She is stunningly beautiful. She carries books in her arms like armour. Her friends, the group, at the table adjoining that of the Mazilli children, try to get her to join them. Acknowledging them with a smile, she signals no, tossing her head back and forth. Slow motion close: Angela. Her hair falls over one eye. As she pulls the stray curl back, her great dark eyes notice Francesco watching her. She returns his gaze. Francesco is enchanted.

Who is she?

TONY
What's it worth to you?

FRANCESCO
Are we the same blood? What's the matter with you?

TONY
So I'll give you a discount.
Angela heads off. Francesco rises and follows her.

FRANCESCO
I'll find out for myself.

DIANA
Sighing cynically
And then there were two.

TONY
So what do we do now?

DIANA
How about you grin, and I'll bear.

EXT. STREETS OF VASTO. EVENING.
Francesco follows Angela at a discreet distance. They play a kind of hide and seek. Through Vasto's streets, Francesco now loses her around this corner, now catches a glimpse of her again at the far end of a square, disappearing down some lane-way. She doesn't know herself followed, or does she? Emerging around a final corner, in a very quiet part of town, Francesco seems to lose her completely. Francesco's gaze comes to rest on the door of an ancient chapel.

INT. CHAPEL. EVENING.
At first, in the darkness, he can see nothing. And then light. Angela has placed some coins in a slot mechanism which illuminates a sixteenth-century painting.

For several moments, she and the painting are illuminated. Francesco watches in awe from behind a pillar as Angela gazes at the painting and makes a few hasty notes. Then the light goes off and the chapel is returned to almost complete darkness, but for the votive candles near the altar. Francesco advances carefully, listening to the chink of her coins. When the light comes on again, he is standing almost beside her. Angela starts.

FRANCESCO
Don't be afraid.
[Non avere paura.]

ANGELA
You're the American, aren't you?
[Tu sei l'americano, vero?]

FRANCESCO
Canadian. There's a difference.
[Canadese, prego. C'è differenza.]

ANGELA
She smiles sceptically.
Why did you follow me here?
[Perchè mi hai seguita qui?]

FRANCESCO
Like you, to study beauty.
[Perchè come te, amo la bellezza.]

She looks away, at the painting, feigning indifference, though obviously pleased. The light goes off again. Both their hands fumble nervously with coins and the slot. When the light comes on again, Francesco boldly takes her hand in his. Angela pulls her hand away and leaves abruptly.

INT. MAZILLI APARTMENT. LATE AFTERNOON.
Maria is folding clean underwear at the card table. The animated sounds of an argument. Maria comes to the

windows to see what's happening. Aerial shot:
Giovanni down in the street, arguing with the two men
in a truck.

EXT. MAZILLI'S SHOES. LATE AFTERNOON.
The two men have their arms folded on their chests,
eyes impassive and half-closed at Giovanni's entreat-
ies. Tony and Francesco join their father in the street.

GIOVANNI
To his sons.
They're on strike. They just heard on the radio.

FRANCESCO
So what are we supposed to do, just wait?

TRUCK DRIVER
You move to Italy? You do this of your own free will? In
Italy, everybody is free to wait. There's lots of waiting here
for nothing.
[Le cose vanno così in Italia; si aspetta per tutto, c'è più
tempo che vita. Nessuno vi ha forzati a tornare in Italia.]
Giovanni looks up at the sky, as if to invoke heaven,
and sees all the windows above him crowded with aged
spectators.

GIOVANNI
Aprite. Open up. We don't need anybody. We'll do it
ourselves.

EXT. MAZILLI'S SHOES. APPROX. ONE-HOUR LATER.
The empty truck drives off, leaving Mazilli and sons
sweating and surrounded with the furniture they have
emptied onto the street.

INTER-CUT VARIOUS SHOTS OF MAZILLI AND SONS.
They are attempting to manoeuvre their Canadian-
sized furniture up the narrow apartment staircase.
Many of the pieces will not fit through the door.

EXT. MAZILLI'S SHOES. DAWN.
> *Mazilli's sleeping face. His head is propped uncomfortably on one arm of the sofa and he is covered in a blanket. An eyelid flutters in the dawn light. His face is stubbled and grey-looking. Pull back to reveal that the sofa is on the sidewalk. Mazilli has slept with their furniture overnight. Further pull back reveals the Vigile in the frame. He is writing out a large yellow ticket, which he hands to Mazilli.*

GIOVANNI
What's this for?
[Ma che state facendo?]

THE VIGILE
Parking in a no-parking zone.
[È una multa per parcheggio non autorizzato.]

INT. MAZILLI APARTMENT. DAY.
> *The sofa, on a pulley, is parallel to a large window, with French-style doors that open out. The boys' arms reach out to receive it. Once the couch is manoeuvred inside, the Mazillis let out a collective cheer. Tony holds one end of the couch, a huge grin on his face.*

TONY
Where do you want it, Mom?
> *We see the grin slowly disappear, as Tony's p.o.v. reveals an apartment over-stuffed with furniture, so that there is barely enough room to move. Maria signals to some improbable location in the room.*

MARIA
There, for now.

VASTO SUPERMARKET. DAY.
> *The supermarket is larger than a Canadian corner grocery store, but considerably smaller than a North American supermarket. It has only the one check out,*

at which Maria and Giovanni are bagging their groceries. They talk freely in English, which gives them an illusion of privacy.

MARIA

It's not your fault. But you're going to have to change your head. We're in Italy now.

GIOVANNI

I know where we are.

MARIA

For hundreds of years these people get their free salami at Christmas from the meat guy, shoes from the shoe guy. In Sicily, they have to pay a fee to the Mafia.
Silence, as twenty heads turn.

GIOVANNI

Shhh. They don't like that word here.

MARIA

Abruzzi is better. But are you going to change what's been going on for hundreds of years? Give away a few pairs of shoes.

GIOVANNI

No. I'll pay my fines. I'll pay my taxes. But no free shoes.
The cashier urges them to bag faster.

CASHIER

Sbrigatevi.
The cluster of customers at the cash has become backlogged. Maria pushes the food toward Giovanni, who throws it into bags.

INT. MAZILLI'S SHOES. DAY.
Giovanni is taking inventory and Tony is vacuuming, when Diana saunters through the shop, a beach bag slung over her arm.

GIOVANNI
Where are you going?

DIANA
The beach.

GIOVANNI
This is Italy, not Canada. A girl does not go to the beach alone unless she's a *puttana*. You understand? Tony, take your sister.
> *Tony gladly drops the vacuum and takes off after his sister.*

VASTO'S SEA SIDE. HIGH SUMMER. DAY.
> *Close shot of the back of Diana in a bikini, picking her way gingerly across the burning sand toward the sea. Pull back to include Tony bringing up the rear. Men of all ages notice Diana and respond to her passing. She is l'Americana, which means an instant and easy popularity. She is approached by a man, who starts wooing her in ardent Italian. Diana looks back and calls to her brother.*

DIANA
You handle it.
> *Tony gets this mischievous idea.*

TONY
> *Whispering to the man.*
What's it worth to you?
[Quanto sei disposto a pagare?]
> *The man, misreading the situation, thinks he is being directed to come to terms.*

THE MAN
Ventimila lire.

TONY
You must be joking.
[State scherzando!]

THE MAN
Still misreading the situation.
Cinquantamila lire.
Diana, appalled, turns around and fixes her kid brother with a look.

DIANA
What are you doing?

TONY
Speculating. *Cinquantamile lire* is — C'mon you're the math whizz.

DIANA
Cuffing him.
For forty-two bucks, you'd sell your own sister?

TONY
I just wanted to see what you'd fetch.

THE MAN
Still misreading the situation.
Centomila lire.
Diana removes her dark sunglasses and fixes the man with a stare meant to douse his ardour.

DIANA
Shoo.
[Pussa via.]
As she replaces her sunglasses, she sees a sophisticated young man watching her from his lounge chair. He has overheard everything and is amused. He gives Diana an approving smile. She smiles back, replaces the sunglasses, and chooses her place on the beach. The young man gets up from his lounge chair and approaches.

INT. MAZILLI'S SHOES. DAY.
Mazilli is meeting with a Milano sales representative from a major shoe manufacturer. The Rep. is all style

— *Bruno Magli shoes, Giorgio Armani suit, borsolino hat. He's a real prince: comes into Mazilli's shop with his trench coat slung casually over his shoulders, tests the shelving with a critical finger, looks over the place with a slightly contemptuous air.*

GIOVANNI

Volete un caffè?

Maria offers an espresso on a silver tray with her finest bone china and biscotti on the side. In the meantime, the rep's assistant has brought in sample shoes in boxes, which the rep. is in no hurry to unlid. The rep's prevailing attitude is very much: you-need-us-more-than-we-need-you.

I want to turn this store into the finest in Vasto, nothing but the best. That's why I arranged for this meeting. I'm looking for exclusivity.

[Vi ho chiamato perchè voglio che il mio negozio diventi il migliore di tutta la città. Voglio l'esclusiva.]

MILANO REPRESENTATIVE

Exclusivity? That will cost you. But for the right price, everything is possible.

[L'esclusiva costa. Ma tutto si può fare.]

GIOVANNI

Can I see the shoes?

[Fatemi vedere il campionario?]

The rep. snaps his fingers and his assistant lifts the lids reverently off the shoe boxes. Giovanni's eyes light up.

EXT. MAZILLI'S SHOES. DAY.

Angle on: the display window. The new shoes are given prominent display in the front window. A customer comes into the store.

CUSTOMER

How much for these shoes?

[Quanto costano queste scarpe?]

GIOVANNI
Trecentomila lire.

CUSTOMER
What? Frediani Calzature has them for $150.
[Ma come, Frediani Calzature vende le stesse scarpe per centocinquantamila lire.]

GIOVANNI
That's impossible. That's less than I paid for them. But come back tomorrow. If it's true, I'll give that pair to you for 10,000 lire less than Frediani.
[È impossibile. Devono essere una imitazione. Lasciatemi indagare su questa faccenda e se quello che dite è vero, vi prometto che io ve le venderò per diecimila lire meno di Frediani.]

> As soon as the customer leaves, Giovanni shouts up to the apartment for Francesco to mind the store. Hastily, he puts on his jacket and rushes across town to Frediani Calzature.

EXT. FREDIANI CALZATURE. DAY.

> Reflected in the glass, we see Mazilli stooped and peering into the display window. Close up of Mazilli's face mirrored in the glass through which the shoes show like a pentimento. Mazilli's face falls as he locates the subject shoes.

INT. A BAR IN VASTO. DAY.

> A depressed Giovanni quaffs two cognacs in rapid succession. A familiar voice rings out.

CABBY
Hey, my friend, did Canada turn you to drink, or is it Italy?

> Giovanni looks around himself, delighted to recognize The Cabby, Antonio Tassista.

How have you been?

GIOVANNI
Depends.

CABBY
On what?

GIOVANNI
The weather, the tourists, the politics. Above all, the politics.

CABBY
What do you mean?

GIOVANNI
I'm supposed to be the exclusive distributor. No one else can sell the shoes. Top buck, I pay, only to find Frediani Calzature is selling the same shoes, and for less. How can Frediani sell the same shoes, when I have exclusivity, and for half the price?

CABBY
Easy.

GIOVANNI
Still uncomprehending.
But how?

CABBY
Stupido. This is Italy. Frediani has a special arrangement. Every month, the Milano guy gets a little something from Frediani and Frediani gets a little something from him.
   The Cabby takes some lire from his wallet and, reaching under the table, stuffs the bills into Giovanni's pants. Continuing.
Capisci?
   The Cabby finishes off his beer and laughs, reaching across the table to pat Giovanni's shoulder.
You'll learn. And when are you going to start selling running shoes?

GIOVANNI
I want to sell quality — Italian quality.

CABBY
This is your problem — you're an American trying to sell Italian shoes to Italians, when what Italians want is American.

GIOVANNI
You stick to your cab; I'll sell the shoes.

CABBY
What can I do for you? I try to teach, but you don't want to learn . . .

EXT. AND INT. MAZILLI'S SHOES. DAY.
Series of shots. Giovanni arranging the shoes in his display window. Giovanni again waiting inside his door. Giovanni scrambling the shoes in his display window and re-arranging them. Giovanni adjusting his tie, leaning inside his door. Maria comes up to him (inside door). Giovanni looks back at empty store, then at Maria, shrugs his shoulders. Giovanni, on his knees inside the shop, surrounded by boxes, removing all the shoes from his display window and replacing them with a whole new display of shoes.

EXT. MAZILLI'S SHOES. DAY.
Giovanni leans inside his doorway. Antonio Tassista pulls up in his cab, gets out and opens the door effusively for the woman seated inside, taking her hand to her great amusement and pleasure.

CABBY
Such a beautiful hand. As delicate as your little feet must be. Such special feet must have special shoes. This is the best shoe store in Vasto.

Antonio Tassista shows off the store like an artist his canvas. Giovanni watches the two approach, his jaw open in amazement.

AMERICAN TOURIST
Greeting Giovanni.
Good day, sir. I want something very Italian.
[Buon giorno, signore. Voglio qualche cosa molto italiano.]

INT. MAZILLI'S SHOES. DAY.
Giovanni tries to please her. He shows her a very simple but elegant pair of Bruno Magli shoes.

AMERICAN TOURIST
But are these Italian?

GIOVANNI
Of course. Look at the lines, so simple yet practical. You want to try them?

AMERICAN TOURIST
They're really Italian?

GIOVANNI
Absolutely. Feel the leather, soft as a baby.
She feels, but dismisses this particular pair.

AMERICAN TOURIST
Show me some more.
Mazilli shows her another pair. The Cabby stands back at first.
Too gaudy.
Another pair.
Too severe.
Then another.
Too tight.
And another.
Heel too high.
Giovanni's mood shifts from over-eagerness to an almost hostile, what-does-she-want? He isn't having

fun selling and she's not having fun buying. Surrounded by boxes, Mazilli tries to ram the American tourist's toes into yet another pair of shoes. O.S. The Cabby announces:

CABBY

Ecco.

Giovanni and the tourist look toward the storageroom curtain. Antonio Tassista appears, dramatically holding aside the curtain with one hand, the shoe box high, in the other. He pushes Giovanni off the stool.

Close your eyes, *mia bella signora.* I want you to be surprised.

Obediently, she closes her eyes. Sensuously, he removes the shoe and hands it to Giovanni with a look which plainly conveys what Antonio thinks of Giovanni's salesmanship. The foot awaits its surprise. Antonio runs his fingertips along the underside of the foot. She giggles and opens her eyes. Antonio guards the box. She closes her eyes again. He dresses her foot in the shoe — red, white and blue sandals, encrusted with three white stars.

And now, *bella signora, guarda* — look at what your own loveliness has created.

AMERICAN TOURIST
Thoughtful pause.

I like these.

She turns her foot first this way, now that, then stands and struts toward the mirror.

GIOVANNI

You like these?

AMERICAN TOURIST
Defensively, to Giovanni.

Yes, I like these.

Lowers her voice and says coyly to the Cabby.

But are they Italian?

CABBY
Inhales deeply.
No one but an Italian could design such shoes.

AMERICAN TOURIST
How will anyone know?

CABBY
Signora, anyone who knows Italians will know.
She sits back and sighs, completely satisfied by this explanation. A maestro bringing to a close a symphony, Antonio removes the shoes, never taking his eyes from the woman's, places them in the box beside him and hands them over to a perplexed and peripheral Giovanni to ring up the sale.
What kind of an Italian are you? And when are you going to sell running shoes?
[Ma che razza di Italiano sei? Ma quando ti deciderai a vendere le scarpe da tennis?]

EXT. BOOKSTORE. DAY.
Angela enters the bookstore. Francesco enters behind her, before the door swings closed, though unremarked by Angela. The woman behind the counter recognizes Angela, and assumes the two are together.

SHOPKEEPER
Finally, Angela. I have not seen that look in a man's eyes since I was twenty!
[Finalmente Angela. Non vedevo uno sguardo così innamorato da quando avevo vent'anni!]

ANGELA
Following the shopkeeper's eyes and meaning:
He isn't with me.
[Ma lui non è con me.]
Angrily, to Francesco:
You again?
[Ancora tu?]

Angela turns around and abruptly leaves the book-
store.

FRANCESCO
To shopkeeper:
What does she read?
[Che tipo di libri legge?]

EXT. BOOKSTORE. DAY.
Francesco emerges from the bookstore with a large
artbook under his arm. Tony, who has been leaning
against the wall waiting for him, mocks him.

TONY
I could have found that out for you at half the price.

INT. BILLIARD HALL. DAY.
Tony approaches the table where young men are play-
ing billiards, watched by their friends. He waits his
opportunity, then announces to the group at large:

TONY
There's a busload of American women arriving tomorrow.
[Domani arriverà un pullman pieno di turiste Americane.]

ENIO
So what?
[E allora?]

TONY
So what? To get inside them, you've got to talk their
language. You understand?
[E allora, per poterle conquistare dovete parlare inglese,
capisci?]

ERCOLE
What's he talking about?
[Ma cosa dice?]

TONY

I can teach you to say things in English that will make them yours. If you speak English, you can score big.
[Vi posso insegnare delle parole in inglese che le farà innamorare. Se parlate inglese, vi prometto grandi cose succederanno.]

ENIO

And how would a little squirt like you know?
[E tu, come lo sai? Hai ancora il latte in bocca.]

TONY

Because I have imagination. And English.
[Perchè ho fantasia. E parlo inglese.]

BRUNO

Yeah? So give us a sample.
[Mm . . . Facci un esempio.]

TONY

You go up to the girl and look at her with your dark, romantic eyes. She sees you looking and that catches her attention. But without the words, you can't make the leap.
[Allora, ti avvicini e la guardi intensamente negli occhi. Lei ricambia lo sguardo. Ma se non dici niente, niente succede.]

Play-acting both the guy and the girl, Tony puts his arm around an imaginary female.

At this point you say to her in English: "Is your father a thief?" "No," she says, surprised. "Then who stole the stars and put them in your eyes?"
[A questo punto tu dici in inglese. "Tuo padre è un ladro?" "Certamente no", risponderà lei, sorpresa. "E allora chi ha rubato la luce delle stelle per metterla nei tuoi occhi?"]

General laughter.

Now you've got her.
[A questo punto, lei sarà stregata.]

Having caught the interest of the men, Tony reels them in, translating sentences into lire. The older boys have

*fun with him, treating Tony's advice half in serious-
ness, half in jest.*
You, what's your favorite solicitation to an American
woman?
[Senti un pò tu, come faresti ad adescare una turista ameri-
cana?]

ERCOLE
C'mon, Enio, let's hear it.
[Dai, Ennio, dicello.]

BRUNO
Teasing, he wipes Enio's brow.
Look at the sweat. He hasn't used his head this much in
days.
[Guarda com'è sudato. Si vede che il suo cervello non è
abituato a lavorare troppo.]

ENIO
Suddenly inspired.
"*Le mie labbra sono come il gelato. Mangiami subito altri-
menti mi sciolgo.*"
General laughter.

BRUNO
You use that? And it works?
[E funziona? Ma che patetico.]

TONY
Encouraging.
That's the idea.
[Sei sulla bona strada.]
Tony translates this request. Continuing.
"My lips are ice cream. Quick, eat me before I melt."

ENIO
Practising, he pronounces the words laboriously.
My lips are eyesa-scream. Eata me before I melt.

ERCOLE

How do you say, "You need a hand into your bathing suit?"
[Come dici, "Ti serve una mano sul tuo costume da
bagno?"]
> *Innocently, as if no double-entendre is intended, Er-*
> *cole accompanies his words with a hand on Bruno's*
> *ass.*

TONY

But only the first one was for free. Now you pay and I'll
tell you.
[L'esempio è gratis. Ma ora devi pagare.]
> *The young man throws him a coin.*

ERCOLE

What a bandit.
[Che brigante.]

ENIO

. . . Eyesa-scream . . .
> *Money in hand, Tony translates.*

TONY

"You need a hand into your bathing suit?"

ERCOLE
> *Practising.*

You need a hand in the bathing suit?

ENIO

My lips are eyesa-scream . . . Shit, I forgot the second part,
tell me again.
[Merda, ho già dimenticato la seconda parte. Ridimmela
per favore.]

TONY
> *Practising with Enio slowly.*

Eat me before I melt.

PANCRAZIO
He's been struggling all this time with the muse.
Listen to this, "You're so sweet, you give me a tooth ache."
[Sentite questa. "Sei così dolce che mi viene il mal di denti."]

TONY
I like it. Short and to the point.
[Bellissima. Corta ma efficace.]
> *Tony indicates to Pancrazio with his hand the need for
> more coin. Receiving it, Tony translates.*
"You're so sweet you give me a tooth ache."
> *In control of his stage, Tony rehearses the guys in their
> solicitation phrases and pockets their lire.*

INT. MAZILLI'S SHOES. DAY.
> *The Cabby barges into the shop accompanied by a
> photographer. What is conspicuously different about
> the shoe store is the rack of running shoes just inside
> the door.*

CABBY
And how is my running shoe department?

GIOVANNI
As a matter of fact, I sold two pair of Michael Jordan this
morning.

CABBY
Overjoyed for his friend.
You see. Did I tell you?
My cousin, Vittorio. He works for the newspaper.

JOURNALIST
Shaking Giovanni's hand.
Nice to meet you.
[Piacere.]
> *Organizing Giovanni, the journalist props him against
> a backdrop of shoes and puts a shoe in each hand.*

GIOVANNI
What's this all about?

CABBY
I've convinced him to do an article: "Italy's returning sons."
You can't buy publicity like this.

GIOVANNI
To journalist.
I left Italy with nothing. Now look at what I've accomplished. When you're young, you do things because you don't know any better. It's not courage, it's just lack of fear. To do this at my age, takes balls.
[Quando sono emigrato non avevo niente. Ma quando sei giovane non hai paura di niente. Niente sembra impossibile. Ma alla mia étà a ricominciare ci vogliono le palle di ferro.]

CABBY
. . . Relax. The less you say, the better. Let him take the picture. The picture's worth more than the words.

GIOVANNI
Compulsively, as if to unburden himself.
When you've been away as long as I have, you see with clearer eyes. After twenty-three years in Canada, I see only too clearly what's wrong with Italy.
[Quando sei stato lontano per ventitre anni, vedi tutto con occhi diversi. Riesci a capire cosa non funziona in italia.]

JOURNALIST
We'll get the picture first, then just a few words to sum up.
[Prendiamo le foto adesso, poi penseremo alla storia.]
> *Close of Mazilli, against the backdrop of shoes. At the last moment, he holds up the shoes. They look for all the world like donkey ears. Flash. The Vasto journalist has taken his picture.*

EXT. VASTO SEASIDE. DAY.

A tourist bus pulls up beside the change cabins; its door opens and young women begin to disembark. The young men from the billiard hall are there to greet them. The scene should play like an onslaught, with much of the dialogue overlapping.

PASQUALE

Do you have any Italian in you?

Beat, as Pasquale puts his arm around the reluctant American girl.

Would you like some?

BRUNO

To girl directly behind her.

If looking good's a crime, you'd be jailed for life.

ERCOLE

To girl directly behind her.

You lovely, lika fly with butter.

ENIO

My lips are eyesa-scream . . .

The american girls react with disgust. Enio falters in mid-line.

AMERICAN GIRL

Calling back toward the bus.

How do you say "get lost" in Italian.

Tony sees a window of opportunity.

TONY

I can translate.

The American girl pats him patronizingly on the head.

AMERICAN GIRL

Isn't this cute. The freak show comes with a midget.

Laughing, the American girls link arms and walk disdainfully toward the beach. The next girl disem-

barks, the word Arizona *emblazoned across her T-shirt, (across one breast).*

ENIO
Calling out to her, as if he knows her.
Arizona.
He rushes her and grabs her hand.
Pleased to meet you. And what's the name of this one?
Pointing toward the other breast.
[Piacere. E tu come ti chiami?]
Terrified, the girl pulls back and climbs back into the bus.

BRUNO
Forget that one. Flat as a board.
[Scordati quella li. Piatta come una scopa.]
The next girl disembarks. She is tall and athletic, with a no-nonsense expression. She walks coolly through the pack, as each tries a different approach.

BRUNO
The moon, she'sa beautiful, ma nothinga lika you face.

PASQUALE
I have a Swiss account and a Ferrari. Can I take you somewhere? Anywhere?

PANCRAZIO
I've read Boccacio. Have you?

ERCOLE
I know people — Tom Cruise.

ENNIO
If it's columns you want, there's more for you here . . .
Cupping his genitals.
. . . than in all of Rome.
They're all ignored. The guys look toward Tony and the mood begins to turn ugly.
It worked better in Italian.

[Funziona meglio in italiano.]

TONY

It's not the translation. The lines were stupid to begin with.
[Non è la traduzione. Le vostre frasi sono stupide.]

BRUNO

So you deliver. Get one for us.
[E allora, inventale tu. E portacene una.]
Enter Diana, who recognizes Tony as the author of the situation.

TONY

You've got to help. They're going to lynch me. Pretend
you're not my sister . . .

DIANA

No way. If I'm going to help, you're going to do it the right
way. No pretenses.

INT. BUS. DAY.
With proverbial cap in hand, Tony tries to explain what happened. Outside the bus, the guys have formed a chorus and are serenading the girls with "Tenimmuci a Cussi," a famous Neopolitan love song. The girls are warming up, as expectation begins to meet reality.

TONY

They were just trying to impress you. They got this Ital-
ian/English dictionary, but it didn't come out right. They're
really sorry. They asked me to ask you if they can treat you
to some ice cream.
Diana nudges him.
On me.

INT. MAZILLI APARTMENT. KITCHEN. MORNING.
Maria and the kids pore collectively over a newspaper article spread across the kitchen table. Tony groans.

*Giovanni enters the kitchen and meets the accusatory
eyes of his family.*

TONY
"Ecco the Prophet Mazilli: head of a bull, balls of a young
man."

FRANCESCO
Whose idea was this?

GIOVANNI
Delighted.
They published it!

MARIA
. . . I bet I know whose idea it was.

GIOVANNI
You can't buy publicity like this.
He rushes to the paper.

FRANCESCO
"Canadian shoemaker thinks he can teach Italians how to
sell shoes."

GIOVANNI
I didn't say it like that.

FRANCESCO
They printed it like that.

MARIA
When are you going to learn people don't wish you well
when you make your choices sound smarter than theirs?

DIANA
They made you sound ridiculous. And this picture: You look
like an ass.

*Giovanni looks up from the newspaper into the hurt
and anger of his family. The momentary pleasure he
felt at the exercise of a brief vanity dissipates on his*

face with the realization of its consequence. He is
genuinely in pain. Beat. Giovanni heads for the door.
He turns and looks at their collective, accusing eyes.
Beat of silence. He leaves. Maria and the kids exchange
concerned glances.

INT. BARBER SHOP. SUNDAY. DAY.
The scene opens with an overhead medium shot of
Mazilli in Sunday clothes, being draped with a protec-
tive bib, his face with the barber's steaming cloth.
Mazilli's face is tired, but relaxed, anticipating the
pleasure of a shave. The camera remains on Mazilli's
draped body, as o.s., we hear town regulars enter the
barber shop and exchange recognitions. The o.s. mur-
mur of voices becomes suddenly louder, as Mazilli's
ears prick to the words "the Canadian." Door bell.
Sound of greetings, door closing.

VOICE O.S.
Hey, Federico, did you hear what the Canadian paid for
DiPasquale's business? Maybe we can convince him to buy
half of Vasto.
[Ei Federico, hai sentito come DiPasquale ha imbrogliato il
Canadese. Forse possiamo convincerlo a comprare mezzo
paese.]

ANOTHER VOICE O.S.
That old fox, DiPasquale. I always said, he shakes your hand
and you have to count your fingers afterward.
[Quel furbacchione di DiPasquale. Ho sempre detto di non
fidarsi di lui, devi stare attento che quando ti stringe la
mano non ti porta via qualche dito.]

FIRST VOICE O.S.
A Canadian with lots of money but no common sense.
[Un Canadese con tanti soldi ma niente cervello.]

VOICE OF THE SCUPINI O.S.
I don't know if he's so rich. His garbage doesn't have as
many meat bones as when they first arrived. I think they
must be eating lots of pasta with beans over there. Business
can't be too good for the Canadian.
[Non so se è così ricco. Non ci sono più avanzi di carne
nella loro spazzatura come quando sono arrivati. Gli affari
non devono andare troppo bene. Scommetto che sono
ridotti a pasta e fagioli.]

Mazilli is as still as stone beneath his drapery. The
barber has done nothing to silence the talk about him.
Camera pulls back to include the barber removing the
cloth from Mazilli's face. Their eyes meet in the mirror
— the barber's a mixture of ridicule and curiosity;
Mazilli's, of anger and a dawning horror at the reali-
zation he's been had.

EXT. STREET OF VASTO, EARLY MORNING.

The Spazzini (garbage men) are at the top of the street
with the Vigile, poring over a newspaper. The one puts
his two index fingers up beside his temples, as if to
signify horns, in clear imitation of the photograph. The
other laughs. The garbagemen advance down the
street, picking up everybody's garbage except Mazilli's.
Giovanni, who has seen all this through the store
window, runs into the street after the Spazzini.

GIOVANNI
Hey, what about my garbage?
[Ei tu, e la mia spazzatura?]

SPAZZINO
Your box is not the right size. It has to be so many centimetres by so many centimetres. And only so many boxes per
family.
[Il tuo bidone non è della misura regolamentare, e ogni
famiglia può usare un solo bidone.]

Giovanni looks down the street. There is no rhyme or reason to the size or shape of anybody's garbage.

GIOVANNI
What about that box, and those bags.
[Ma non è vero, guardate a tutte le altre famiglie, c'è chi usa anche sacchetti di plastica.]
The garbage man folds his pudgy hands across his stomach and closes his eyes like a cleric.

SPAZZINO
It's written, it's the regulation.
[Non ci posso fare niente, è il regolamento.]

GIOVANNI
Where is it written?
[E dove sta scritto?]

SPAZZINO
Indignant.
You think I'm paid to answer your stupid questions? Go ask the Mayor.
[Ma tu pensi che a me mi pagano per rispondere alle tue stupide domande. Se non ti piace, vai a parlare col Sindaco.]

INT. CITY HALL. DAY.
We see a long and crowded reception corridor, chairs on either side, people waiting patiently with various parcels on their laps — a purse with an ill-concealed prosciutto sticking out, a satchel with a large round of cheese. Giovanni, accompanied by Tony, bursts upon this resigned scene through swinging doors followed by a gaggle of excited functionaries. Giovanni's footsteps are loud and determined (Tony's stride matches that of his father, in miniature); the gestures of the func-tionaries are as wild as they are ineffectual to stop them. Giovanni bears before him in his strong arms the infamous box of garbage, tied with a pink bow. The group passes through a second set of doors, leaving

*silence in its wake. All eyes watch the door. Several
beats, then the box of garbage is hurled back into the
corridor and bursts on impact with the marble floor.
Giovanni follows, physically thrown from the Mayor's
office. He picks himself up under the eyes of the
reception room and his son Tony, who has been spirited
from the Mayor's office by the scruff of his neck. Tony
watches with embarrassment as his father, avoiding his
son's eyes, brushes garbage from his clothing, straightens himself, and tries to walk down the corridor with
the same dignity as he walked up it.*

INT. MAZILLI KITCHEN. NIGHT.

*Mazilli is alone at the kitchen table, which is strewn
with books of account. Several empty espresso cups
indicate he's been at this for hours. Sleepily, Maria
comes into the room wearing a dressing gown. She
places her hands on Giovanni's shoulders and begins
rubbing his neck tenderly.*

MARIA

How bad is it?

*Giovanni takes Maria's hand and holds it in both his
own. Instinctively, his fingers find her wedding band
and play with it like a worry bead.*

GIOVANNI

The only thing selling are the running shoes.

INT. VASTO TRAIN STATION. MORNING.

*Angela has just purchased her ticket and passes through
the paned-glass station doors, surrounded by a gaggle
of well-dressed relatives. We can tell from the body
language of this distracting little crowd that the gist of
their animated conversation is a flood of well-meaning
admonishments on the one hand, and an indulgent
and weary, sì, moma, sì, Zia Rosa, on the other from
Angela. Against this backdrop, Francesco approaches*

the wicket to purchase his ticket. His body language indicates the direction of Angela on the platform. The attendant leans forward to follow Francesco's drift. With a complicitous wink, the ticket attendant eagerly facilitates Francesco's wish, selecting a ticket beside an empty slot. Francesco purchases his "ticket to Angela." He boards the train quickly just as Angela separates from her crowd.

INT. FIRST CLASS TRAIN COMPARTMENT. DAY.

Francesco is seated beside the window with his legs casually crossed, an art book open and concealing his face. Angela enters the compartment and takes her seat directly across from him. She proceeds to do what anyone would in a comparable situation — unguardedly takes her fellow occupant's measure. She notes the book's subject with interest. As the train pulls away from the station, Angela waves goodbye to her people. Francesco closes the book and looks out the train window, giving Angela an opportunity to arrange her face. Recognition is accompanied by a brief flush of pleasure, followed immediately by anger at the thought she has been manipulated. She rises to leave. All pretence vanishes. Francesco catches her hand.

FRANCESCO

I'll find another seat. You stay here.

[No, non te ne andare. Cambio posto.]

Angela takes pity on him and sits down. They travel together in silence, Angela looking out the window while Francesco gazes at her.

ANGELA

What did you think we would talk about for three hours?

[Di che cosa volevi parlare per tre ore?]

FRANCESCO

Di te. Di che cosa mangi la mattina, del profumo che usi,
qual'è il tuo colore preferito . . .

> *As Francesco's spontaneous list of questions grows*
> *longer, the words competing with themselves for her*
> *attention, Angela begins to laugh.*

ANGELA

Stop. Stop. In English, at least, so I can practise, since you
must be here.

FRANCESCO

. . . What you ate for breakfast this morning, what perfume
you wear, your favourite colour, whether you bathe at
night, or in the morning? I want to know everything about
you, *tutto di te.*

ANGELA

Are all Canadian men like you?

FRANCESCO

What am I like?

ANGELA

Not Italian. Italian men only like to talk about themselves.

INT. UFFICIO POSTALE. DAY.

> *Giovanni and Tony wait in line at the post office with*
> *a parcel for Nonno Leone for his birthday. Giovanni*
> *fidgets nervously.*

GIOVANNI

What's everybody staring at? Never seen a man with a
parcel before?

TONY

Nobody's looking.

GIOVANNI

He's looking. She's looking.

Close of faces. A man looks over his reading glasses. A woman lowers her book and fixes Giovanni with her eyes.

TONY

Sure if you talk loud and point, people are going to look.
Their turn comes at the wicket.

GIOVANNI
Taking pains not to ruffle feathers.
Can you weigh this parcel, please. I need to buy stamps.
[Può pesarmi questo pacco, per favore, e darmi i francobolli?]

POSTAL CLERK
Wrong lineup.
[È nella fila sbagliata.]
The Clerk signals Giovanni over to a line just as long as the line they've just waited through.

GIOVANNI
What do you mean it's the wrong line up? That man just bought stamps here.
[E allora come mai ha venduto i francobolli a quello prima di me?]

TONY
Cool it, Dad. You're making a scene.

GIOVANNI
Persistent.
I saw him. What's the problem with me?
[L'ho visto coi miei occhi. Chi sono io lo scemo del villagio?]

POSTAL CLERK
Looking past him.
Next?
[Desidera?]

TONY

It's the wrong lineup, it's the wrong lineup. Just accept.
Taking his Dad's arm and pulling him over to the second line.

GIOVANNI

No, it was the right line. It's just the wrong line for Mazilli.

TONY

What are you talking about?
They take their place at the back of the second line.

INT. UFFICIO POSTALE. LATER.
Giovanni gets to the second wicket.

POSTAL CLERK NO. 2

Your parcel is not supposed to be wrapped like this. You need a different kind of paper and string, and a special seal. [Il pacco non deve essere sigillato così, bisogna usare la carta da pacchi.]

GIOVANNI
To Tony.
You see? You see?
To clerk.
Where do I get this special paper and seal?
[E dove la compero la carta da pacchi?]

POSTAL CLERK NO. 2

Across the street, there's a tobacconist who sells it.
[Dal Tabaccaio di fronte.]

GIOVANNI

And this tobacconist, is he your cousin? What do you get for your vigilence?
[E il tabaccaio è un vostro parente? Vi spartite il guadagno?]

POSTAL CLERK NO. 2
Confused.
What?

[Come?]

TONY
Wait in line. I'll pick up the paper.

EXT. STREET OF VASTO. STILL LATER.
Tony crosses the street toward camera. Moments later we see the backside of Tony returning to post office, trailing string and a roll of paper under his arm.

INT. UFFICIO POSTALE. STILL LATER.
An anxious Mazilli waits mid-way through a lineup, looking back toward the post office door for Tony. Tony arrives and, hastily, they wrap the parcel as prescribed.

INT. MAZILLI'S SHOES. DAY.
Maria is minding the shop alone. A lady arrives.

MARIA
Buon giorno.

LADY CUSTOMER
Buon giorno.

MARIA
And who do I have the pleasure of serving?
[E chi ho il piacere di servire, signora?]

LADY CUSTOMER
I'm the wife of the Chief of Police.
[Sono la moglie del Commissario.]

MARIA
Ah.
The lady selects a pair of shoes.

LADY CUSTOMER
How much for these?
[Quanto costano queste?]

MARIA
Don't worry.
[Non si preoccupi.]
Maria packs up the shoes with an air of distraction.

LADY CUSTOMER
Why?
[Perchè?]

MARIA
Don't worry, take the shoes, a gift.
[Non si preoccupi, le prenda, omaggio dei Mazilli.]
The wife of the chief of police, gratified, takes the shoes
and goes away. She says from the door:

LADY CUSTOMER
Thank you. And welcome to Vasto.
[Grazie. E benvenuti a Vasto.]

INT. UFFICIO POSTALE. LATER.
Their turn at the wicket has arrived again. Mazilli
presents his wrapped parcel.

POST OFFICE CLERK
What's inside?
[Cosa contiene il pacchetto?]

GIOVANNI
It's none of your business.
[Niente di illegale e niente che vi riguarda.]

TONY
Just tell him.

GIOVANNI
A present for my father-in-law, for his birthday, and a
birthday card.
[Un regalo per mio suocero per il suo compleanno e un
biglietto di auguri.]

POST OFFICE CLERK

Number one, you're not supposed to wrap it up. You have to wrap it up in front of that woman at that wicket. Number two, no cards on the inside.

[Prima di tutto non dovete mai avvolgerlo con la carta da pacco. Questa operazione va fatta davanti all'impiegato postale. E secondo, non potete inserire nessun biglietto.]

Giovanni tries to control the hysteria in his voice.

GIOVANNI

But there has to be a card, for Canadian customs, so in case they open it in Canada, they know it's a gift.

[Ma se non c'è un biglietto come fa la Dogana Canadese a sapere che è un regalo?]

Disinterestedly, the man signals for the next customer, who shoves Giovanni aside.

INT. UFFICIO POSTALE. STILL LATER.

In the third line, Mazilli angrily unwraps the parcel, muttering to Tony.

GIOVANNI

He says no card. And he wants to see with his own eyes what we're wrapping. They've got it in for me. The whole town's in this together.

TONY

Get real, Dad. Just go with the flow, we'll get out of here faster.

Deftly, Tony takes the little card, scrupulously folds it, and tucks it into the instep of the leather shoe that is his Nonno's birthday present.

INT. UFFICIO POSTALE. STILL LATER.

Giovanni and Tony are at the third wicket. Giovanni has broken into a sweat. Tony is as cool as a cucumber.

FEMALE POSTAL CLERK

Open the box, please.

[Aprite le scatola per favore.]
> *Giovanni opens the box with trembling hands and watches nervously as the postal clerk lifts the tissue paper and shoes.*

O.K., you can wrap it up now.
[Bene, adesso potete avvolgerla nella carta e legarla.]
> *Giovanni wraps it up in front of her and hands the parcel over to her to be weighed, almost blowing it with nervousness. She takes the parcel, puts it on a conveyor belt of parcels headed back behind the counter to wicket number two.*

You pay the postage over there.
[Per i francobolli dovete fare la fila allo sportello numero due.]
> *Giovanni looks in despair at the first lineup.*

GIOVANNI
You see. It's deliberate. They're out to torment me.

TONY
Haven't you heard — when in Rome? We're not the only ones in line. Don't take it personally.

INT. FLORENCE TRAIN STATION. DAY.
> *Francesco and Angela disembark. Angela clutches her hand luggage, with the purposeful air of one seeking now to distance herself from her travelling companion. She heads toward the end of the platform where a political demonstration is taking place. Unexpectedly, policemen enter the station; demonstrators carrying placards scatter. A demonstrator runs past Angela, hurling his placard aside. It catches the side of Angela's hand. She cries out and Francesco is at her side. He throws his arm around her and whisks her out of harm's way. In the safety behind a column, Angela looks back toward the confusion of the platform, her breathing still panicked.*

FRANCESCO
Why do you always run from me?

ANGELA
Why do you follow?
[Perchè mi segui?]

FRANCESCO
You don't know yet?

ANGELA
You're not for me.
[Non fai per me.]

FRANCESCO
How can you say that? You don't even know me.

ANGELA
I know. A woman just knows. You are wrong for me.
[Lo so. Una donna sa queste cose. Sei sbagliato per me.]

FRANCESCO
Then I promise to be the best mistake you'll ever make.
[Ti prometto che sarò l'errore più giusto che hai mai fatto.]
*Francesco lifts Angela's hand to his lips and reverently
licks her blood. Astonished, Angela just watches him.
There follows a wordless silence. Her blood glistening
on his lip, Francesco looks into Angela's troubled eyes,
his expression one of hopeless adoration.*

INT. MAZILLI'S KITCHEN. EVENING.
*The family is having dinner. Missing is Francesco.
Looking distracted, Giovanni mutters discontentedly.*

GIOVANNI
The Italian postal system stinks. As bad as it was in Canada,
we could still get a letter across the country in three days.
Enter Francesco, looking excited.
Is this a hotel?

FRANCESCO
I did what you suggested. I went exploring. I'm going to
Florence, Dad — to study.

GIOVANNI
Just like that. No discussion?

FRANCESCO
It's what you wanted. I'm going to become an engineer.

GIOVANNI
Why Florence?

FRANCESCO
It has a private university.

GIOVANNI
But there are closer universities. Less expensive.

TONY
Teasing his big sister.
. . . Who's the guy with the beard?

GIOVANNI
What's Tony talking about? What guy?

DIANA
Reluctantly.
A student.

GIOVANNI
A student? How old is this guy?

DIANA
I don't know.

TONY
He looks about twenty-four.

GIOVANNI
Twenty-four? He's too old for you.

DIANA

I'm not a child anymore. I can do what I want.
Giovanni brings his fist down on the table.

GIOVANNI

You're still my daughter. This is still my house.

DIANA

Raising from the table.
You made me leave one man to come with you to Italy. What
do you want to make me, an Italian nun? Will that make
you happy? Do we all have to live your life?
She runs to her room in a tearful rage.

GIOVANNI

Maria, control your daughter.

FRANCESCO

Control yourself. Look at you —

MARIA

Francesco, he's your father.

FRANCESCO

But it's true. Look at him. His anger is not with us. It's with
himself. He's been at war with Italy, ever since we arrived.
I'm the only one here who is trying to love Italy.

GIOVANNI

Italy? It's a woman, isn't it. You've found a woman.
Francesco doesn't deny it.

GIOVANNI

He's in love with a woman, and he thinks it's Italy.

FRANCESCO

The woman is Italy. Your shoes are Italy. The teller in the
bank who serves you last because you won't give him two
thousand lire, is Italy. You don't know Italy. You don't know
yourself. You don't even know why you came.

GIOVANNI
Giovanni confronts the hurt and anger of his family.
I did it for you.

FRANCESCO
You did it for yourself. Everything you've done, you've done for yourself.
Giovanni stands, suddenly, sending his chair crashing. Silence. As if unable to breathe, Giovani clutches at his shirt. He turns from his family and leaves suddenly. The Mazilli family looks after him in despair. They hear the shop bell tinkle and fall silent as the door down-stairs opens and closes behind him.

MARIA
He succeeded in getting what he wanted.
[È riuscito ad avere quello che voleva.]

EXT. VASTO. EARLY EVENING.
Mazilli walks through the streets of Vasto, alone. The hour of the passeggiata is drawing to a close. People are wandering home to the evening meal in groups of twos and threes. Giovanni passes a parkette where a group of elderly men linger around a concrete table, finishing their game of cards. Giovanni hesitates a moment to watch them from a distance. We know from the way he looks at them that he is thinking of his cronies back in Canada. He turns away finally and continues walking. Giovanni rounds another corner. He looks around in bewilderment, or disorientation, as if he has stumbled upon something he did not expect to find — his own past. Giovanni sees through a window a mother serving soup to her son. The boy is seated at the head of the table. Giovanni appears transfixed by the scene.

INT. ROOM. EVENING.

There should be a magical, warmly-tungsten quality to the light in the room. The boy and the mother appear dated in their clothing — late 1930s or early 1940s — the boy in short pants and a sweater. Perhaps it is simply their poverty that dates them or makes them appear timeless. For all their poverty, they seem happy. The mother wears a flower in her hair. She is deferential, almost flirtatious, to the small boy who sits at the head of her table like a little adult, breaking the bread and passing it to his mother.

EXT. STREET. EVENING.

The street has grown dark around Giovanni. His eyes glisten with tears in the reflected light from the window.

SEASIDE. VASTO. NIGHT.

Mazilli walks beside the ocean, alone. The lounge chairs are folded, the umbrellas closed. Mazilli walks at a quickening pace. He is hyperventilating, as if in a state of panic. Voices reverberate in his head, echoes of things he himself has said and the voices of others, until he thinks he'll go crazy from the crush of them all.

FRANCESCO

. . . You did it for yourself. Everything you've done, you've done for yourself.

GIOVANNI

. . . There's nothing here for me anymore.

LUCIANO

. . . There's nothing there, either.

GIOVANNI

. . . I can't live here anymore.

MARIA
. . . Then you can't live anywhere.

GIOVANNI
. . . Then I can't . . .

NONNO LEONE
. . . He never had a stomach for strangers' food.

GIOVANNI
. . . What strangers? I'm going home.

NONNO LEONE
. . . Home? *Che cosa è questa fantasia?*

MARIA
. . . Italy is finished. Why can't you just accept?

FRANCESCO
. . . You did it for yourself. Everything you've done you've done for yourself . . .

Camera follows Giovanni as he breaks into a run. The only sounds We hear are the ocean and Mazilli's panicked breathing.

EXT. SEASIDE. DAWN.

Close of Mazilli's sleeping face. He is curled on a lawn chair, beside a stack of folded chairs and umbrellas.

TONY O.S.
Dad. Hey, Dad.

Mazilli's eyes flutter, then snap open. Recognizing his son, he reaches out and embraces Tony tightly.

EXT. A HILL. DAY.

Aerial shot: Mazilli strides up the side of a hill, the panting Tony struggling to keep up to his determined father.

TONY
Where are we going?

GIOVANNI
You'll see. A history lesson. You should know something of the blood you come from.

At the crest of the hill is a graveyard. Giovanni pauses, breathing heavily. He shades his eyes with his hand, stares at the graveyard, then back at the town of Vasto, spread at their feet.

EXT. GRAVEYARD. DAY.

Italian graveyards are sociable places. Built around courtyards like miniature replicas of crowded cities, the graves rise above ground in concrete miniature apartments. Each filing cabinet bears the photograph of its occupant, gregariously facing the occupant across the way. Giovanni's p.o.v.: Out under the dazzling sun, Tony walks up and down the rows, looking at the graves. Background sounds of trickling water and cicadas. Giovanni cups his hand under a tap of water used for tending flowers and drinks thirstily.

GIOVANNI
To himself.
Where's the little cemetery I remember?
Tony calls to his Dad.

TONY
I think I've found them.

GIOVANNI
In the same haunted voice, almost to himself.
Show me.

INT. GRAVEYARD. DAY.

Tony's and Giovanni's p.o.v.: two gravestones. The photographs of Giovanni's parents are inconsistent, from much different times. The photograph of his mother is of a sad-looking old woman. His father is a romantic-looking young man, eyes gazing off into space.

GIOVANNI
It was the only picture we had of him. He never stayed in one place long enough to have his picture taken. I don't remember ever being a kid. I had to be the little man of the house when he was gone, but when he came back, one wrong word and my ears would sing with the back of his hand . . . I must have hated him.

TONY
You look a lot like him.

GIOVANNI
You think so?
Giovanni shivers, as if, the fever lifted, the cold of his night beside the sea has finally entered his bones. Practically.
I wonder if I could make them change this picture of my mother. It doesn't seem fair he should be young forever.
Giovanni stands back and takes a picture of his parents' graves.

TONY
Are we going home?

GIOVANNI
Home? Why?

TONY
Weird — like tourists take pictures. Why take a picture of something you can see just the same tomorrow?
Giovanni puts an affectionate arm around his son's shoulders.

GIOVANNI
It's never the same tomorrow. What am I talking about? I'm talking nonsense. Your father doesn't know anything anymore. *Non ha senso più niente.*

EXT. A STREET CORNER IN VASTO. DAY.
Giovanni, returning to town with Tony, bumps into the Commissario, who happens to be with the Vigile. The Commisario is almost cloying friendly to Giovanni.

COMMISSARIO
Hey, Giovanni, *tutto a posto?*
Giovanni is confused, but pleased.

GIOVANNI
Not bad. And you?
[Non c'è male. E voi?]

COMMISSARIO
By the way, thank you very much.
[A proposito, grazie tante.]

GIOVANNI
For what?
[Per che cosa?]

COMMISSARIO
The beautiful shoes. My wife loves them.
[Le bellissime scarpe. A mia moglie piacciono molto.]
Close of the Vigile's face as the realization dawns that the Commissario has been given preferential treatment. Giovanni hopes to repair what he thinks must be a misunderstanding.

GIOVANNI
Did my wife Maria give her a discount?
[Mia moglie le ha fatto uno sconto?]

COMMISSARIO
Hey, what a discount!
[E sì, e che sconto!]
The Commissario winks and pats Giovanni on the back which leaves no doubt. Giovanni burns with humiliation and rage. As they leave, the Vigile turns to

*pin Giovanni with a vicious little look of which they
alone know the significance.*

INT. MAZILLI'S SHOES. DAY.
*Giovanni storms into the shop which Maria is minding
alone, while taking inventory. It is empty of customers.*

GIOVANNI
How could you do this to me?

MARIA
Do what?

GIOVANNI
Behind my back. To give away shoes . . .

MARIA
Me? To you? What I've done to you? Look—
*Maria pulls open the drawer under the cash register
with such fury that it falls to the floor, strewing papers
about. She reaches down, picks up a fistful of yellow
tickets and waves them at Giovanni.*
Twenty-three years. This is twenty-three years? Look, I've
never told you what to do. I can even understand why you
did it. I have myself to blame, as much as you. What we've
done, we've done. No regrets. But think now . . .
Giovanni is cowed by her anger.

GIOVANNI
. . . I'll think. I'll think — about the free shoes.

MARIA
I'm not talking now about free shoes. It's gone beyond free
shoes.

GIOVANNI
Then what are you talking about?

MARIA

Italy doesn't want you anymore. You left, she was like a woman who had loved you, only you couldn't see it. You left, but kept looking for her somewhere else . . .

GIOVANNI

. . . I'm confused.

MARIA

. . . You couldn't love Canada because you couldn't get over Italy, and in your arrogance, you thought all you'd have to do is return to her and she would take you back again, as if nothing had happened. It's too late.

Just as she says so, the bailiff troops in with two men. The men proceed straight to the back of the store and start removing shoe boxes in armfuls. At first, Giovanni is stunned. When the bailiff's man plucks a shoe box from Giovanni's hands on his way out the door, Giovanni snaps into action.

GIOVANNI

What's going on here?

[Che succede qui?]

The impassive bailiff stands with his sheaf of official papers, ticking off his own inventory.

THE BAILIFF

You haven't paid your fines.

[Non avete pagato le multe.]

GIOVANNI

They're under protest.

[Le sto contestando.]

THE BAILIFF

First you pay, then you argue.

[Prima pagate e poi discutete.]

GIOVANNI
I'll pay them today. But leave the shoes where they are. How can a man pay if you rob him of his business?
[Le pagherò oggi. Ma non portatemi via le scarpe. Come posso pagare se non posso vendere?]
> *Giovanni is frantic. He tries alternately to bar the door and to pluck boxes away from the men as they head for the truck parked just beyond the door. But the parade is ineluctable.*

THE BAILIFF
You'll get the shoes back when you've paid the fines.
[Le scarpe vi saranno restituite quando avrete pagato le multe.]
> *The bailiff licks his thumb and index fingers, slowly rips a long official sheet off his pad and hands it to Giovanni. The shelves are empty. The bailiff politely closes the door behind him. It has all happened so quickly. Giovanni and Maria stand silently side by side, staring out the now-empty shop window: misery and dismay in Giovanni's every feature, acceptance and perhaps a sense of vindication in Maria's. We hear the truck drive off.*

GIOVANNI
Today, I'll go . . .
> *Giovanni's voice breaks.*

MARIA
Don't go anywhere. You're wasting your time. Let's go back to Canada before we have no country to return to.
> *Close up of Giovanni's face, tears of rage and disappointment in his eyes, then a look of recognition as his eyes narrow and come into focus on the man across the street.*

EXT. STREET. DAY.

> *Long shot of the Vigile standing across the street. He has seen and, in Giovanni's eyes, is responsible for everything.*

INT. MAZILLI'S SHOES. DAY.

> *Close shot of Giovanni. All of Giovanni's disappointment and anger come to focus upon the Vigile, whose gesture has been like waving red to a bull. Follow on Mazilli, as he runs out of the shop after the Vigile.*

EXT. STREETS OUTSIDE MAZILLI'S SHOES. DAY.

> *The Vigile's first impulse on seeing Giovanni is to turn and run. But Giovanni grabs him by the scruff of his neck and pant belt and spirits him toward the town fountain at Vasto's heart. He hurls the Vigile into the fountain. Then Giovanni scrambles in after him to make sure he finishes the job: now dunking him, now hauling him up for air, singing above the man's gasping shouts for help like a woman doing her laundry.*

GIOVANNI
Vola, vola, Vola.

VIGILE
Help. Help.
[Aiuto, Aiuto.]

> *Giovanni dunks with one hand. With his free hand he directs an imaginary choir of voices in this famous song from the Abruzzi region. We see townspeople run toward the fountain. Music swells above the Vigile's howls: "Vola, Vola, Vola . . ." children surround the fountain and join in the singing.*

EXT. MAZILLI'S SHOES. DAY.

> *The Cabby drives his cab onto the sidewalk in front of Mazilli's Shoes and throws open the door. Seizing his window of opportunity, he runs into Mazilli's Shoes*

*and emerges with the running shoe stand and runners
slung about his neck. He begins hawking:*

CABBY

Mazilli shoes, Mazilli shoes, only *ventimila lire.*
[Le scarpe di Mazilli, le scarpe di Mazilli.Solo ventimila
lire.]
He spots Tony Mazilli.
Tony, help me help your father.
*Together, they dart in and out of the crowd like peanut
vendors at a ball game, and the townspeople sponta-
neously begin shelling out lire for their souvenirs.*

INT. POLICE STATION. A CELL. NIGHT.
*A sodden Giovanni is shivering on a cell bench. The
door opens, shedding light upon Giovanni's isolation.
Sheepishly, he looks up at Tony, Diana and Maria, who
have arrived with the bail money and a blanket.*

EXT. POLICE STATION. NIGHT.
*As they leave the police station together, Giovanni puts
a blanketed arm about Maria's and Tony's shoulders.*

GIOVANNI

How did you get me out?

MARIA

The Commissario.
She adds coyly.
He remembered the free shoes.

GIOVANNI
Teasingly.
I hope you gave some to the *parroco* too, so the Priest won't
tell our sins.
Maria and Giovanni both laugh.

EXT. VASTO STREETS. NIGHT.

We follow Giovanni, Maria, Diana and Tony as they round a corner of Vasto's empty and darkened streets and break into the moonlit square where the fountain spews water in isolated splendour. Unexpectedly, Giovanni begins to sing, at first humming and then singing in full voice the same song he sang while dunking the Vigile. His mood becomes one of almost wild elation, building again toward the climax of that afternoon in the town square, the echo of the Vigile's screams, the shouts of merchants running from their shops. Tony and Diana join into the song with their father, the two of them singing and laughing. Tony jumps up onto the rim of the fountain, balancing himself with outstretched arms. Maria laughs with her family despite herself.

MARIA

Are you all crazy?

GIOVANNI

Ah, Maria, you should have heard him spluttering about in that fountain, so helpless without his little ticket book.

TONY

Everyone's talking about you, Dad. Everyone's saying he's had it coming for years.

GIOVANNI

I'd have done it all over again, anyway, no matter what they say. It was worth it. I'd do it again, tomorrow, no matter how many times the bastard fined me. No regrets.

Maria squeezes her husband with both arms circled about his waist and presses her face lovingly against his chest.

MARIA

No regrets.

Giovanni encircles her with both arms, so that she is lost in the blanket, in the memory of their youth. Echoing her, Giovanni's voice is a loving whisper meant for Maria alone.

GIOVANNI

No regrets.

He kisses her on the lips.

Moments later: Francesco, arm around Angela, rounds the corner and comes upon this scene of his father, brother, sister and mother by the fountain. The couples stare at each other in amazement. Then a shivering Giovanni, looking like Moses in his blanket greets his son from across the piazza.

Francesco, we're going home. You'll come with us?

Francesco presents Angela to his family.

FRANCESCO

I love a woman. The woman is here.

Giovanni is amazed that all this has happened, without his knowledge.

GIOVANNI

Am I your father? I don't deserve to be told?

FRANCESCO

Gently.

Let go, Dad. You're not angry with me. It just didn't happen the way you expected.

Maria goes up to Angela and wordlessly embraces her. Then she touches her son's face.

MARIA

I promised you, I would ask of you only once. Now you belong to yourself. And to this beautiful woman.

Maria takes a hand from each of the young lovers and gives them her blessing.

Love her like your father loved me.

[Amala come tuo padre ha amato me.]

GIOVANNI
Almost to himself.
Am I stupid? I got what I wanted. I should be happy for
him. Francesco, you have done what I wanted to do. You
will be the one to enjoy Italy. And I? — I leave my blood,
something of myself, here in Italy.
Everyone embraces.

INT. BLUE BIRD CAFÉ. DAY.
Giovanni's cronies are playing cards and talking.

THE PHILOSOPHER
Life is like a melon. When you open it, you don't know
whether it's going to be sweet and ripe, or tasteless like a
cucumber.
[La vita è come un melone. Può uscire rosso ma può uscire
anche bianco.]
*Shot widens to include Mazilli, playing cards with his
cronies.*

GIOVANNI
Old man, I didn't understand you before I left. I still don't
understand you. There are some things I will never understand. *Scopa.*
*Giovanni throws his card down in obvious delight at
winning the game. His cronies register disgust at losing
yet another. Enter Sam.*

SAM
Ancora, Mazilli?

GIOVANNI
What?

SAM
You never learn?
*Sam signals toward the window, where Mazilli's car is
being front lifted by a tow truck. Giovanni rushes off,*

as cronies laugh.Credits up and over the following. To the music of "La Casetta in Canada."

SHOT OF WHITE WALL, ABOVE A CAPPUCCINO MA-
CHINE, INT. BLUEBIRD CAFÉ.

A man's hand enters frame and positions a nail in the middle of the wall. The other hand enters frame and hammers in the nail. Then, both hands lift a large, framed photograph into frame and centre it. It is the photograph taken by the Vasto journalist of Mazilli, posed grandly against the background of his shoes.

END

Printed and bound
in Boucherville, Quebec, Canada by
MARC VEILLEUX IMPRIMEUR INC.
in October, 1999